The Jaguar's Children: Pre-Classic Central Mexico

by Michael D. Coe   The Museum of Primitive Art, New York

Distributed by the New York Graphic Society, Greenwich, Connecticut   1965

Copyright 1965
The Museum of Primitive Art
15 West 54th Street
New York, New York 10019

Library of Congress Catalogue Card Number: 65-15714

Design: Hiram Ash

Contents

PREFACE

This monograph is based upon materials assembled for an exhibition of early central Mexican art which was held at the Museum of Primitive Art from February 17 to May 5, 1965. I would like to join with the Museum in thanking the lenders to the exhibition. Their generosity and goodwill were very much appreciated; the aid of Mr. Everett Rassiga was indispensable. I also wish to thank Mr. Carlo Gay for providing illustrations of the Chalcatzingo relief, and Miss Julie Jones, of the Museum's staff, for assistance in the preparation of this study.

INTRODUCTION

The Classic civilizations of Mexico and adjacent Central America were presaged by a long developmental period, the Pre-Classic, that lasted from about 1500 B.C. to A.D. 250. It is the middle part of the Pre-Classic that concerns us here, the span from 800 to 300 B.C. during which the spectacular Olmec culture existed side-by-side with a variety of lesser peasant groups scattered throughout Mexico.

Central Mexico is an upland region formed mainly by a great volcanic cordillera extending from east to west. Not far to the north is the enormous central desert of the country which reaches the Texas frontier. To the east lie the lowland plains of the Gulf Coast, lush and tropical with fertile soils. A chain of volcanoes reaches west almost to the Pacific coast. Rolling away to the south are the highly dissected mountains and hills of Oaxaca, homeland of the Mixtec and Zapotec.

The main centers of population in Central Mexico have always been the broad and well-watered valleys, particularly the inland basin known as the Valley of Mexico, a mile and a half high and covering 3,000 square miles. With few exceptions, this land is now relatively dry and treeless, green in the summer but turning to dust in the long winter. We have every reason to believe that conditions were much different in the Middle Pre-Classic:[1] the level of the now-desiccated Great Lake in the Valley of Mexico was as high as it has ever been, and oak forests probably reached from the rolling hills and mountains above the valley almost to the swampy margins of the water. Deer roamed through wooded plains where now factories belch their fumes into the smog of 20th century Mexico City. Innumerable water fowl—ducks, geese, herons and many other species—thronged the surface of the Great Lake. All available evidence points to a climate considerably wetter and more favorable for early settlement than that of today.

Situated to the south and southwest of the rim of volcanoes that border the Valley of Mexico are the plains and valleys of Morelos and adjacent Puebla. The altitude of these lands is considerably lower, between about 3000 and 6000 feet, and even today the climate is semi-tropical compared to that of the Valley. The heat and humidity make it possible to grow in its fertile volcanic soils many kinds of tropical fruits, and under irrigation even such a crop of the Old World tropics as sugar cane. One can assume that the Morelos-Puebla region was more lush during the 800-300 B.C. time range. In contrast to the Valley of Mexico which has no external outlet, the Morelos-Puebla region is well drained, particularly by the headwaters of the Río Balsas, which eventually winds its way through the State of Guerrero and to the Pacific.

In such favorable surroundings, it is little wonder that central Mexico attracted early agricultural settlers. Very primitive hunter-collectors domesticated corn in the Mexican highlands by the beginning of the fifth millennium B.C., and squash before that. The basic triad of native Mexican farming and diet—corn, beans, and squash—was being grown by many peoples in the region at the beginning of the first millennium B.C. Pottery, weaving, and other arts of settled life were then present among the village farmers.

By the early years of this century it was known that there had been pottery-using peoples in central Mexico before the advent of the great Classic civilization of Teotihuacan. Their remains had been dubbed "Archaic," a term now reserved for the pre-pottery, incipient agricultural period which preceded it. The real discovery of the Pre-Classic cultures was principally the achievement of the late George C. Vaillant, in a series of excavations conducted for the American Museum of Natural History from 1928 through 1932.[2] These concentrated upon three early villages, located in ancient times on the northern shore of the Valley of Mexico: Zacatenco, Ticoman, and El Arbolillo. Through stratigraphy and typology of pottery and figurines Vaillant was able to show that the deepest levels of El Arbolillo were the oldest in the Pre-Classic Valley sequence; Zacatenco began slightly after this; the later Ticoman was occupied until just before the initiation of Teotihuacan civilization. As adhered to by most students of the subject today (but not by all!) Early and Middle Zacatenco and El Arbolillo I and II would be considered Middle Pre-Classic, and Late Zacatenco and Late Ticoman as Late Pre-Classic.

The way of life of the Middle Pre-Classic villages must now be considered. Marked by a peasant simplicity, it led Vaillant to believe that these villages were not the most primitive of their kind and must have been preceded by cultures on a lower level, yet they were by no means the match of the Classic civilizations that followed.[3] He therefore called all of the Pre-Classic phases the "Middle Cultures." Middle Pre-Classic pottery is simple in shape and decoration; tens of thousands of handmade, solid pottery figurines from El Arbolillo and Zacatenco represent nude females, perhaps part of a farmer's fertility cult. Few if any of the deities of Classic Mexico are recognizable. The crude graves at Zacatenco held no offerings, while the better-made slab lined graves of El Arbolillo contained at the most a few pots, or an obsidian blade or other tool. No temples, temple platforms, or other hint of but the most rudimentary social or religious hierarchy was found.

A hint of difference came from a site outside the Valley of Mexico itself. This was Gualupita, excavated by George and Susannah Vaillant in their last season of work on the Pre-Classic cultures.[4] Gualupita was a stratified village and burial ground discovered by brickyard operations on the north side of Cuernavaca, Morelos. The topmost levels produced material quite clearly dating to the period between the Teotihuacan culture and the Aztec conquest. Below was a Pre-Classic occupation which contained many of the same figurine types seen previously at Zacatenco and El Arbolillo. However, the burial offerings at Gualupita were superior in number and in workmanship to those of the Valley of Mexico sites, both in pottery and in figurines. Among the ceramics was an unusual group of gadrooned bottles, incised neckless jars, and whiteware dishes with gutter spouts. Two large, hollow clay figures were unlike anything yet seen in the Valley of Mexico: they had puffy, infantile facial features, and mouths drawn down at the corners. The Vaillants immediately identified them as representing the "'babyface' style of sculpture in Southern Mexico."[5]

The recognition of such a sculptural style had been the accomplishment of Marshall Saville. In 1929 he noted that a number of objects with baby-faces merging into snarling jaguar visages, a cleft often at the top of the head, could be traced to the lowlands of Veracruz and neighboring states. Since the area was traditionally

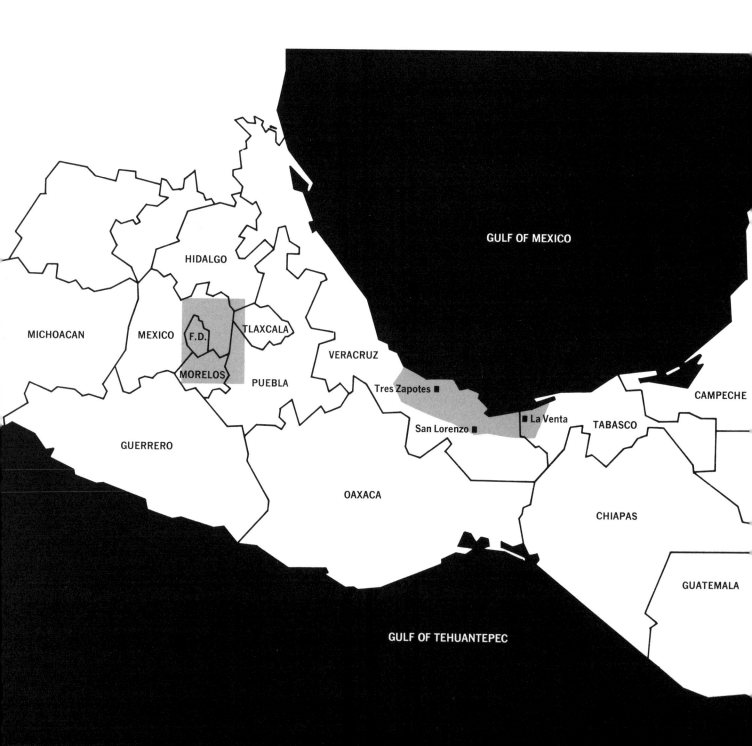

Map of Mexico, indicating central highland area and Olmec "heartland" along the Gulf Coast.

Map of central Mexico.

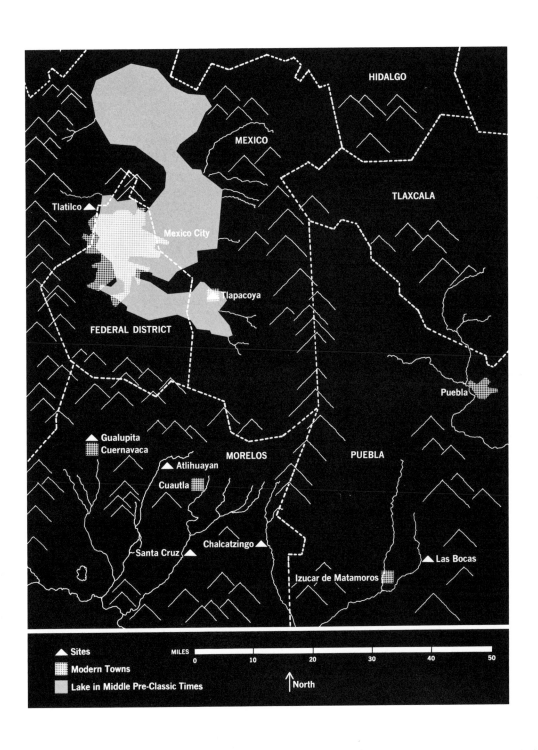

Sites

Modern Towns

Lake in Middle Pre-Classic Times

MILES

0   10   20   30   40   50

↑ North

HIDALGO

MEXICO

TLAXCALA

Tlatilco ▲

Mexico City

Tlapacoya

FEDERAL DISTRICT

Puebla

Gualupita ▲
Cuernavaca

MORELOS   PUEBLA

Atlihuayan ▲

Cuautla

Santa Cruz ▲   Chalcatzingo ▲   ▲ Las Bocas

Izucar de Matamoros

occupied by the "Olmeca," Saville, followed by Vaillant, assigned the name "Olmec" to this new culture. Thus, in his excavations at Gualupita, Vaillant had uncovered and identified Olmec-style objects in a Pre-Classic village. The significance of this discovery both to the chronology of Olmec civilization and to understanding of the complexity of Pre-Classic culture in central Mexico will be examined later.[6]

"Tlatilco" is a name well known to everyone with an interest in Mexican art and archaeology [1, 2, 3]. It was applied by Miguel Covarrubias to an extensive Pre-Classic village site on the lower slopes of the Cerro de los Remedios, on the northwestern outskirts of Mexico City. In ancient times Tlatilco was a very large community, or cluster of communities, on a small stream not far from the shores of the Great Lake. It was discovered through the operations of brickyard workers. There is a strong correlation between Pre-Classic village sites and brick factories in Mexico. Over many generations the clay used by early peoples on the walls of their huts became deposited in such concentration that it could be exploited for brick-making in modern times. By 1942, due to the richness of its finds, it was clear that Tlatilco merited careful excavation, and archaeological work began under the auspices of the Instituto Nacional de Antropología, directed by Miguel Covarrubias and Hugo Moedano Koer. Subsequent work has been undertaken by Moedano in 1947, by Piña Chan in 1949, 1950, and 1955, and by Romano in 1962-64.[7]

In the recorded excavations to date, Tlatilco has produced more than 330 burials, almost all accompanied by offerings of the greatest beauty and sophistication. The taste for Tlatilco pottery and figurines among private collectors and museums has stimulated a lively but illegal exploitation of the site by the brickyard workers. Over the last 25 years it is probable that many thousand additional graves have been pillaged for their treasures. Studies of the grave offerings of Tlatilco have shown it to be like Gualupita but on a much larger scale; furthermore, it is clear that both sites are part of a larger complex, one that spread over more than the Valley of Mexico alone. While probably contemporary with part of El Arbolillo and Zacatenco, Gualupita and especially Tlatilco were not mere peasant villages, but centers of a culture perhaps developed under foreign influence.

This foreign influence was Olmec. Covarrubias purchased two purely Olmec figurines, one of pottery and the other serpentine,[8] at Tlatilco. He came to the not unreasonable conclusion, although one running counter to the then prevailing opinion, that the great Olmec civilization was on the same time level of Tlatilco, or rather, that it was also Pre-Classic. His compatriot Alfonso Caso made the same deduction on the basis of the heavy Olmec influence discernible in the "Danzante" sculptures of Pre-Classic Monte Alban. The Olmec civilization was by this time well-known, through the explorations and excavations of Matthew W. Stirling on the humid Gulf Coast plain[9] at Tres Zapotes in Veracruz, and La Venta in Tabasco. He had uncovered an ancient and highly developed complex which centered on the construction of high temple mounds of clay; an elaborate sculptural style featuring a part feline, part baby-faced, god; colossal heads and other basalt monuments of great size; and beautifully carved jade and serpentine figurines. On the basis of the famous Stela C at Tres Zapotes, which bore a

Long Count date of considerable antiquity, and in agreement with Caso and Covarrubias, Stirling concluded that the Olmec civilization was older than the Classic period, and that the "Olmec" had invented the elaborate calendar and other traits for which the Maya were later famous.[10]

Subsequent investigations in central Mexico have tended to confirm the picture of early Olmec influence or even hegemony over this area. The Olmec reliefs of Chalcatzingo, Morelos, were first described by Eulalia Guzman in 1934,[11] and although she apparently did not realize their true character she suggested they might be identified with "Olmeca" peoples. Excavations made there by Piña Chan led him to conclude that the Chalcatzingo reliefs were associated with a Pre-Classic Olmec occupation of the site.[12]

In the last few years some spectacular finds have been made in Central Mexico by professional pot-hunters, finds which enlarge our knowledge of the Pre-Classic period. Tlapacoya had been an island of volcanic origin in the southeastern part of the Great Lake, although now it is part of the mainland. A major Pre-Classic village exists under the modern town on its ancient northern shore. The only controlled excavations ever carried out there revealed a well-stocked tomb belonging to the end of the Late Pre-Classic period or even to the Proto-Classic.[13] An unknown number of burials belonging to an earlier part of the Pre-Classic have been looted over the past ten years, resulting in the discovery of pottery figures in Olmec style. The latest of the great Pre-Classic burial grounds to be discovered is Las Bocas, near Izúcar de Matamoros in the hot-lands of western Puebla. Las Bocas is said to be a featureless site in a field, not too distant from the little village of Epatlán; its nature is probably only known to local looters and antiquity dealers, but it seems to have been, like Tlatilco, an open village site without mounds, the sub-floor burials in such great concentration that they appear to constitute a "cemetery." Las Bocas rivals Tlatilco in the beauty and excellence of its grave offerings and, as will be shown, forms with the latter and with Gualupita a single cultural complex of the Middle Pre-Classic.

1   View of the brickyards at Tlatilco in 1946.
2   Burials at Tlatilco, 1962-64.
3   Burials at Tlatilco, 1947-50.

10

1

2

3

4   Standing figure holding a were-jaguar. Provenience
unknown, believed to have been taken to Europe during the
19th century. Jade, 8⁵/₈″ high. The Brooklyn Museum L47.6

CHRONOLOGY OF THE MIDDLE PRE-CLASSIC IN CENTRAL MEXICO

The central Mexican sites which have produced the material with which we are concerned—Tlatilco, Gualupita, Las Bocas, Chalcatzingo, and at least part of Tlapacoya—belong principally to the middle range of the Pre-Classic period. The arguments in justification of this statement are typological and chronological, and need not be gone into in detail here.[14] Ever since Vaillant's day, the relative chronology of the Pre-Classic cultures of Mexico and Central America has depended upon the careful construction of ceramic and figurine typologies, and the cautious comparative analysis of stratigraphic columns from different sites and areas. A division of the Pre-Classic of the Valley of Mexico and nearby regions into an Early, Middle and Late was explicit in the later work of Vaillant. More recent research in other parts of Mexico and Guatemala, particularly at Chiapa de Corzo and in the vicinity of Ocós, Guatemala, has suggested that Vaillant's earliest ceramic cultures in the Valley of Mexico might better fall into his "Middle," and that both should be considered Middle Pre-Classic. This does not preclude the possibility that a bona fide Early Pre-Classic may yet be found in the Valley, but it has not materialized thus far, with the possible exception of the Tlálpan phase. The Middle Pre-Classic would thus comprise Vaillant's Early and Middle Zacatenco, and El Arbolillo I and II, with the proviso that Early El Arbolillo I stands at the beginning of the period.

Both Muriel Porter and Roman Piña Chan[15] have demonstrated that almost all the burial goods from Tlatilco can be assigned to the same relative chronological position as Middle Zacatenco and El Arbolillo II, in the latter part of the Middle Pre-Classic. There are difficulties, however. First, Vaillant's stratigraphic technique was grossly inadequate, since he excavated in arbitrary levels of up to several feet in thickness and often must have confused "natural" strata as well as fine changes in the cultural material of the sites which he dug. Secondly, Vaillant was more concerned with figurine typology than with pottery in working out his relative chronology for the Pre-Classic; figurines are extremely rare in proportion to potsherds in these sites, and the possibilities of accidental redeposition or other disturbances in the position of the few figurines must have blurred the real picture. Figurines usually have a much narrower distribution than pottery styles, and are less useful in working out really broad-scale relative chronologies applicable to wide areas. Most confusing of all, many of the kinds of vessels and figurines from the Tlatilco graves are not duplicated in the refuse at El Arbolillo, Zacatenco, and Ticoman.

In an effort to straighten out these discrepancies, Piña Chan made several stratigraphic cuts in the refuse of Tlatilco and on the slopes of the adjacent Cerro de Atoto. His results were comparable to those of Vaillant, but more fine-scale. Three phases were worked out: Early, Transitional, and Late Tlatilco. By his analysis of 1,158 vessels from the Tlatilco burials, he concluded that the grave material belongs in Transitional and Late Tlatilco; Early Tlatilco would then correspond to Early Zacateno and Early El Arbolillo I, which is approximately the same correlation proposed by Porter. None of the burials would therefore be as tardy as the Late Pre-Classic. Further stratigraphic work at Tlatilco by Paul Tolstoy provides additional support for this placement.[16] This would then explain the puzzle of why the grave beigaben of Tlatilco is different from the refuse surrounding the burials: the refuse is Early Tlatilco for the most part and thus predates the burials.

It has been said that Gualupita and Las Bocas are identical in content with the grave furniture of Tlatilco. As far as the former is concerned, Vaillant's arbitrary levels were so large-scale that again little reliance can be placed on his assignment of specific Gualupita graves to phases. Vaillant assigns some of the graves containing Tlatilco-like material to Gualupita II, which he aligns with the Late Pre-Classic culture at Ticoman, but none of the objects in these graves—such as bottles—are known to occur at all in that site. It is obvious that all of the graves are within the Middle Pre-Classic period, coeval with Tlatilco graves, and probably should be called Gualupita I rather than II. This would be apparent anyway from an analysis of the pottery and figurines.

The overall picture then is this: the Middle Pre-Classic opens in central Mexico, as in the rest of Mesoamerica, with a heavy preponderance of white-slipped ceramics, especially flat-bottomed bowls with engraved and excised decoration. Shortly thereafter, the subperiod of the Middle Pre-Classic represented by the Tlatilco, Gualupita, and Las Bocas burials begins. This subperiod is characterized by the following ceramic traits: 1) gadrooned bottles 2) stirrup spout jars 3) bowls deeply excised with the "paw dragon" motif 4) Kaolin ware 5) incised and excised neckless jars 6) animal-effigy vessels 7) anklet-rattle effigy-foot jars 8) plain rocker-stamping 9) white-rimmed black ware bowls 10) spouted dishes. Figurine types include D1, D2, D3, K, and C5. Finally, Olmec influences are strong, and actual Olmec objects are present.

Possibilities exist for an even finer chronology of the Middle Pre-Classic of central Mexico. John H. Rowe and his students, following the example of A. L. Kroeber, have worked out for the South Coast of Peru a fine-scale relative chronology based upon the seriation of grave lots from that region, as well as a seriation derived from the designs and shapes of polychrome pottery. The several hundred recorded burials of Tlatilco could be seriated in a similar fashion; but since the grave associations have not been published in their totality, this could only be done in the Museo Nacional de Antropología in Mexico City. It is my impression that Burials 5, 22, 148, and 196 are late in the sequence; the earliest grave furniture is characterized by the "paw-dragon motif," and by bottles with excised hand-paws and cross-hatching.

The far-flung relationships of the Tlatilco-Gualupita burials have been worked out by Porter.[17] The great ceremonial center of La Venta, Tabasco, the type site of the Olmec civilization, bears clearcut ceramic resemblances, especially in gadrooned bottles. Relationships also exist in art and iconography.

Radiocarbon determinations from the Pacific coast of Guatemala, from Chiapa de Corzo in Chiapas, from La Venta on the Gulf Coast, from various sites in the Peten, and from the Tehuacán valley have led most students to conclude that the Middle Pre-Classic lasted from about 800 to 300 B.C. Two charcoal samples from Tlatilco, each from a burial vessel, are dated at 982 B.C. $\pm$ 250 (M-661) and 567 B.C. $\pm$ 250 (M-660). Given the statistical range of variation, they are well within the time span suggested by Middle Pre-Classic dates from elsewhere in Mesoamerica. The Tlatilco, Gualupita and Las Bocas cemeteries would then be coeval with the apogee of Olmec civilization in the Veracruz-Tabasco lowlands.[18]

On the basis of the collections that I have seen, I believe that Tlapacoya is only partly contemporary with the Gualupita-Tlatilco Complex. Most of the pottery and figurines from that island site probably come from the initial part of the Late Pre-Classic, by which time La Venta was in eclipse and the Olmec impetus had passed to the late center of Tres Zapotes.

OLMEC ART AND ICONOGRAPHY

The Olmec, the great civilization first recognized by Saville and Vaillant, and brought to full light of archeological knowledge by Stirling, is, with the Chavin of Peru, the oldest in the New World. There are several ways of looking at the "Olmec problem." One school holds that Olmec is "just an art style" which happened to be shared over a very wide area of Mesoamerica. This school assumes that there is no connection between a particular art style and the culture of the people who possessed it. Apart from this untenable proposition, there are conflicting views about the origin of the Olmec civilization itself. Small objects in Olmec style are admittedly common in the northeastern part of the state of Guerrero, and Covarrubias thought the Olmec originated there. For other reasons, Piña Chan has leaned to Morelos in central Mexico as the Olmec homeland. The majority opinion would place the initial flowering of Olmec culture in the region where its greatest sites are found, and within which almost all of its great stone monuments are concentrated: southern Veracruz and westernmost Tabasco, aptly termed by Drucker the "Olmec heartland." During the Middle Pre-Classic, the great centers of La Venta, San Lorenzo, Río Chiquito, Potrero Nuevo and Laguna de los Cerros were built as religious and political capitals of the Olmec civilization, and it is upon the content of these sites that the definition of such a civilization can be made.

The Olmec of the "heartland" were great carvers in basalt and andesite, jade and serpentine. An important feature of the powerful Olmec style is its "classicism"—figures stand free in space rather than being surrounded with the clutter of costume and other details characteristic of later, more "baroque" styles like those of Izapa or the Maya. The Olmec artist eschewed straight lines, placing emphasis upon curves which might be considered logarithmic, resulting in a kind of slow-motion monumentality in even the smallest carved object.

Central to the iconography of Olmec art is the concept of the were-jaguar. An extraordinary monument from Potrero Nuevo[19] shows a woman copulating with a jaguar, a representation which Stirling suggested was part of the Olmec myth: the origin of a race of part-human, part-feline infants resulting from such a union. Typically, the were-jaguar [4, 5, 6] is shown with bald head cleft at the top, from which maize or other vegetation may sprout; the narrow or oval eyes are slightly crossed, with full size or eccentrically-placed pupils; above the eyes may be wide brows with flame-like scrolls at the top; the nose is flat and infantile; the corners of the mouth are drawn down in a snarl or cry, the upper lip is prominent and almost hoop-shaped, and the toothless gums have the medial alveolar ridge so noticeable in human babies; occasionally two

long feline canine tusks may curve down and out from the upper gums, and these may have cleft ends; the chin is full and puffy. The body of this monster is that of a sexless, rather obese, human. There is a whole spectrum of were-jaguar forms, ranging from fairly straightforward jaguars, to personages with just the slightest trace of jaguar features. Even depictions which must have been actual portraits—for instance, the "Wrestler" from Minatitlan[20]—show hints of the down-drooping were-jaguar muzzle.

The meaning of the were-jaguar to the ancient Olmec is clear. Covarrubias constructed a kind of family-tree scheme [7] in which all of the well-known rain gods of Mesoamerica—Tlaloc of the Aztec, Cocijo of the Zapotec, Dzahui of the Mixtec, Tajín of the Totonac, and Chac of the Maya—may be traced back to the Olmec were-jaguar, thus definitively establishing the nature of this being. More correctly, all these rain gods were lightning deities who annually brought the rain with the great summer thunderstorms of the tropics. Moreover, the jaguar is an animal closely associated with water in the minds of people like the Maya—he is shown in the codices with a water lily sprouting from the head—a logical idea since this cat does much of his nocturnal hunting along water courses and swims well. The association of a human infant with rain recalls the annual sacrifice of little children to the god Tlaloc among the Aztec; Sahagún tells us that the more they cried, the more auspicious the sacrifice. A clearcut case of sympathetic magic, the tears of the hapless children called down the tears of the heavenly cumulus clouds. That the were-jaguar, monstrous combination of great cat and weeping baby, offspring of human mother and feline father, should have been a rain god is not surprising.

It is apparent that there were several different kinds of were-jaguar, not just one. One of the variations on this theme is bearded. The Olmec could have had different rain gods for each of the points of the compass, just as Tlalocs of different color were assigned to the four cardinal directions among the Aztec.

Second in importance to the were-jaguar in Olmec "heartland" iconography is a bird, or perhaps several different kinds of bird. One is certainly an eagle. Another is a duck, again a creature with water associations; the most striking depiction of it is Monument 9 at San Lorenzo.[21] The shape of a hollow duck has been carved on the front of the breast with a small duck flapping its wings [9]. The idea of an anthropomorphic bird, notably present on the Tuxtla Statuette and later monuments of the Early Classic in southern Veracruz, can be seen in a small basalt monument from Laguna de los Cerros;[22] this has the body of a crouching man, but the wings of a bird [8].

Olmec art has a repertory of symbols and the meanings of some are conjectural. As might be expected, various distinctive features of the were-jaguar—cleft, flame-brow, muzzle, etc.—are used as iconographic elements in their own right. The paw or hand of the were-jaguar, with squared spiral or fret in the palm and with claws extended out and up, was one of these elements. The wings of the anthropomorphic bird from Laguna de los Cerros are so carved that the spiral represents the coverts and the claws the primaries; the same concept can be seen on the sides of Altar 1 at La Venta.[23]

5 *Ceremonial axe in the form of a were-jaguar.*
   Provenience unknown. Stone, 11⁵/₈″ high.
   British Museum, London
6 *Were-jaguar head. Provenience unknown, acquired in 1901.*
   Stone, 6¼″ high.
   American Museum of Natural History, New York 30/9762

5

6

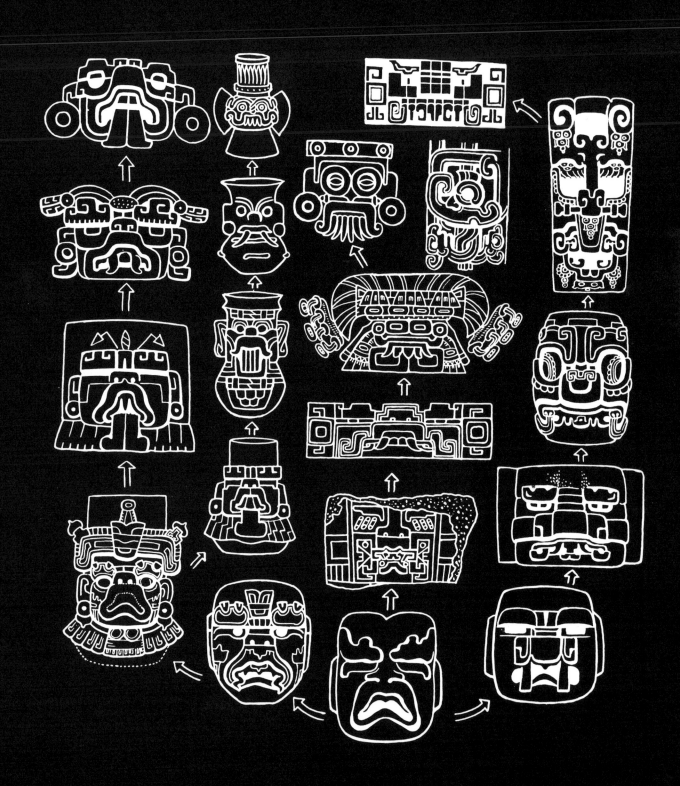

8

9

7

7   *Derivation of Mesoamerican rain gods*
     from the Olmec were-jaguar. Miguel Covarrubias drawing

8   *Anthropomorphic bird from Laguna de los Cerros, Veracruz.*

9   *Detail from Monument 9 at San Lorenzo, Veracruz.*

Two geometric elements occur with great frequency in Olmec art: the crossed-bands motif and the U-element. Among the Classic Maya the former was a glyphic element with the meaning of "sky" and "serpent," almost surely derived from the markings on the back of a snake. Could it have had the same reference among the Olmec? Representations of snakes are not unknown in the "heartland," notably Monument 19 from La Venta, on which a personage is seated in the curved body of a large serpent which may have been feathered. In the Mayan languages—the Olmec may well have spoken an early form of Mayan—the words for "sky" and "serpent" are homonyms, thus explaining in part the association. The U-element is as ubiquitous as the crossed-bands motif; it may be bracket-shaped, like an inverted croquet-hoop, or it may have tapering or slightly outflaring ends. Some of the famous colossal heads from the "heartland" bear it on the headdress. It must be ancestral to the Maya glyph for the moon (T. 683), which has much the same form.

MIDDLE PRE-CLASSIC ART IN CENTRAL MEXICO

The style and iconography characteristic of the Olmec civilization spread, I believe, during the Middle Pre-Classic from the "heartland" in which they had elaborated to the highlands of central Mexico. There they profoundly influenced the simpler village cultures of the region. By the latter half of the Middle Pre-Classic, Olmec artistic ideals coexisted with the native traditional styles. A quickening of artistic excellence in funerary objects resulted from cross-fertilization between these styles. Both artistic streams will be examined here.

Large-scale stone sculpture

The only truly monumental Olmec rock carving yet discovered in all of central Mexico is at the site of Chalcatzingo, near Jonacatepec, Morelos. Rising several hundred meters from the featureless plain are several denuded basalt hills, one of which is the steep-sided Cerro de la Cantera, a striking double-peaked formation looking like a sacred mountain of the Australian aborigines. Several important petroglyphs have been carved on its northwestern side near ground level; all are in the purest Olmec style, indistinguishable from that of the "heartland" of Veracruz-Tabasco.[24]

Petroglyph 1 [10, 11] represents a seated personage placed within what appears to be a mouth and/or cave. This containing band ends in cleft elements, and stylized vegetation (maize?) sprouts from the joints of the band. The personage wears the short Olmec cape and carries in his arms a "ceremonial bar" closely resembling the bar borne by the Olmec were-jaguar in the A. B. Martin collection.[25] His towering headdress recalls that of the left-hand figure on Stela 3 at La Venta. To the right of the figure, scroll-like volutes extend out as though representing clouds of smoke issuing from a cave. The entire scene has been executed to take advantage of the natural relief of the rock. Above the scene are what must be three thunder clouds, rain streaming below, approximating the rain-cloud motif of the Southwestern Pueblos. Further stylized rain drops are scattered between the clouds and the central scene, and can be found in the headdress of the principal figure. They should also be compared to the tears below the eyes of the were-jaguar face on the reverse of Stela C at Tres Zapotes.[26]

Petroglyph 2 [12] has a more martial aspect. Two persons wearing Olmec were-jaguar masks brandish sword-clubs above a bound and ithyphallic captive who is propped up against what might be a statue of a were-jaguar. To the left another masked figure carries before him a staff which seems to sprout vegetation. All three standing figures wear standard Olmec costume: tall headdresses, back capes, and heavy belts with circular devices attached in front.

Petroglyphs 3 and 4 have only recently been discovered. The former is an extraordinary depiction of two fearsome jaguars, each in rampant posture attacking a man. Petroglyph 4 has only partially been uncovered, but according to information kindly supplied by Carlo Gay and Frances Pratt, the subject is a saurian being, perhaps the first known representation of an Olmec Earth Monster. Other lesser petroglyphs were described by Eulalia Guzman, but published illustrations are difficult to interpret.

Olmec reliefs of similar style are known from Padre Piedra in Chiapas, from San Isidro Piedra Parada in Guatemala, and from Chalchuapa in El Salvador. Yet the only free-standing figure in pure Olmec style outside the "heartland" was found to the north of the Cerro de la Cantera at Chalcatzingo.[27] This is a headless, mutilated basalt sculpture of a seated personage with the crossed-bands device on the chest and a wide cummerbund-like belt from which falls the free end of the loin cloth. A comparable monument in the "heartland" is Mounment 23 at La Venta.[28]

11a

11b

11c

11a, b, c   *Details of Petroglyph 1 at Chalcatzingo.*

10   *Petroglyph 1 at Chalcatzingo, Morelos.*

    (Approximate Scale: ³/₄" = 1')

12 a

12a,b Details of Petroglyph 2 at Chalcatzingo.

12 b

Small-scale stone sculpture

Small stone carvings from Pre-Classic central Mexico are almost as scarce as those on a monumental scale, compared with the finds in the "heartland" or in Guerrero. One distinctive but enigmatic object is the so-called *yuguito* ("little yoke"). Several definitely come from Tlatilco, while others in private and public collections may have the same provenience; a few are said to be from Guerrero, and one even from Las Flores, Honduras, but none are known thus far from the Gulf Coast. Alike in shape and similar in dimensions — they are U-shaped, domed objects, the concave side somewhat flattened at its apogee, and the convex surface recurved laterally outwards. The convex section, drawn from the side, would describe a bell-shaped curve. Heights vary from $3\frac{1}{2}$ to $7\frac{1}{2}$ inches. The material is either basalt or andesite. There are probably many plain examples, such as the one bought by Peterson and Horcasitas[29] at Tlatilco, but the majority in collections are carved on the convex surface. The simplest have one large or two smaller concave disks raised from the background. A fine example said to be from Tlatilco has geometric curvilinear designs [13].

The most elaborate *yuguitos* are those with human faces, such as a curious piece with an open mouth and one empty eye socket [16]. Neither this nor an unusual *yuguito* in the Heeramaneck collection [14] showing a human figure lying on its belly and peering through a hole are in a recognizable variation of the Olmec style, but a basalt *yuguito* from Tlatilco in the Dumbarton Oaks collection [15] is certainly Olmec. It bears a powerfully carved were-jaguar face; below the down-drawn mouth is a goatee indicated by the same kind of crosshatching used on carved and excised pottery of Tlatilco graves.

There is little agreement on the use of *yuguitos*. Superficially they appear to be prototypes of the later "yokes," known to represent the heavy protective belts worn in the ballgame. It has also been suggested that *yuguitos* were thigh or elbow guards in the same game. Miss Julie Jones has raised the interesting possibility that they might have represented wooden or leather objects which were bound to the back of the hand and are therefore early forms of the ballgame hand protector. They do fit well to the hand in this position; moreover, the flange-like outcurving on the lateral edges would have served to hold the bindings. A D2 pottery figurine from Burial 129 at Tlatilco[30] shows a ball player wearing such a protective device on the right hand, providing support for the Jones theory.

Jade and serpentine objects are remarkably rare in Pre-Classic central Mexico. None have been found in a controlled excavation at Tlatilco, but Covarrubias purchased a superb Olmec serpentine figurine from a workman at that site. A few other Olmec jade pieces are said to come from Tlatilco: a "stiletto" or punch [18] — in Guerrero and other parts of Mexico these usually represent hummingbirds — and a beautiful head from a figurine [17]. A less recognizably Olmec bead in the form of a head is ascribed to Tlapacoya; several other small Olmec pieces including one of onyx seem to be from Las Bocas. The scarcity of Olmec jade and serpentine in central Mexico, in contrast to its ubiquity in the "heartland" and in Guerrero, will be examined later.

Pottery vessels

The two traditions of central Mexico during the Middle Pre-Classic — the Olmec and the native peasant cultures — are well represented in the several thousand vessels recovered from Tlatilco and other important sites of the period. Most patently Olmec of all is that called here Calixtlahuaca ware [19, 20, 21, 28], first reported by Garcia Payon[31] in Pre-Classic levels at that site in the Toluca valley. This fine pottery is restricted in shape to cylindrical, flat-bottomed bowls, and is coated with a slip which fires white to buff. A smudging material could be placed in zones which were to be darkened, and there is a technical affinity with the white-rimmed black ware so typical of the Olmec "heartland." The designs are usually incised, and show two or three Olmec were-jaguar heads [19, 20, 21] in profile; certain details, such as the upper gums, are crosshatched. Some substitute a more abstract design, perhaps standing for the spots on a jaguar's hide [28], for the were-jaguar head. The center of manufacture of this distinctive ware is unknown. The vessels come from Morelos and from Tlapacoya, but are absent from Tlatilco which suggests a time slightly later than the occupation of the latter site.

Dark Channeled ware may occupy an early position in the development of the Middle Pre-Classic in the region [23, 24, 26, 27, 29, 30, 31]. These vessels are black or brown in color with polished surfaces; the shapes are either round or vertical-walled bowls with flat bases, or bottles. Decoration was in relief, wide flat grooves or channels carved from the burnished surface, excised areas left rough and coated with red cinnabar. There are essentially two designs: 1) the hand-paw theme seen on the anthropomorphic bird from Laguna de los Cerros [26] and 2) the motif identified by Covarrubias as the jaguar-dragon profile and hand design [29]. The latter is the more common, and is a reduction of well-known features of Olmec iconography — a were-jaguar head faces right, with stylized flame-brow above, while to the left is the hand-paw motif employed as the wing of the Laguna de los Cerros creature. A crossed-bands motif may be substituted for the "wing" [31]. Dark Channeled ware is frequent in what are probably early burials at Tlatilco;[32] it occurs at Las Bocas, Tlapacoya, and at Chalcatzingo; and I have picked it up at Río Chiquito in the Olmec area. It is not inconceivable that it was imported from the "heart-land" by the peoples of central Mexico.

Various kinds of polished-excised bowls and bottles may be associated with Dark Channeled ware in place of manufacture, and they certainly occur together in some sites [25, 32-37]. These often have such Olmec designs as the crossed-bands or hand-paw motifs, carried out in such a way that the cut-away and gouged-out areas contrast with polished zones. Flat-bottomed bowls in this style may have bolstered rims. An unusually fine piece in the Michael Kan collection has a roughened band carved in a mat-like pattern [25]. A sensitively fashioned black bottle seemingly stands on its own platform of crossed bands [35]. Red cinnabar or hematite pigment was universally rubbed into the matte areas on these vessels.

The more common bowls and bottles of Tlatilco are brown or reddish brown, sometimes with areas slipped in red [38-46]. On the bottles, gadrooning or grooving with patterns of triangles filled with slanting parallel lines is characteristic, and it is not unusual to find composite bottles which represent double-chambered gourds or a bottle standing on a necked jar [41]. Such grooved and gadrooned bottles, and open and closed bowls bearing incised triangle designs, are the common pottery of such sites as Tlatilco and Gualupita, and in all likelihood of Las Bocas also. Stirrup-spout bottles [43], often with a red-on-buff slip, are found in the Tlatilco burials. They have stirred much controversy since Porter[33] proposed them as part of a larger complex shared by the Chavin culture of Peru and Pre-Classic central Mexico. All of the Tlatilco pieces have flaring-rim spouts, more like those of Valdivia in Ecuador, and the bodies are trapezoidal in cross-section, while Chavin examples are usually round. Multiple and even doughnut-shaped jars [40] are known from Tlatilco, although they are rare. Another curious red or red-on-buff bottle from Tlatilco represents the foot and rattle-covered ankle of a dancer [46].

From Tlatilco and Las Bocas comes an extremely fine-paste, white pottery known as Kaolin ware [47-54]. Most shapes are constricted, neckless jars or *tecomates* and composite silhouette bowls. Puzzling examples of this ware are the little flat-bottomed dishes with gutter spouts [48, 49], which closely resemble Old World libation bowls; this analogy may not be far-fetched, for Sahagún tells us that in Aztec times libations of *pulque* were poured before the hearth in honor of the gods. The infrequent decoration on other vessels may be a red slip [52, 53] or a kind of smudging which leaves a design by the removal of a resist substance [51]. In technique and in beauty of shape, Kaolin ware is perhaps the most elegant of all Middle Pre-Classic pottery from Mexico.

Of immediate appeal to most observers are the animal-effigy vessels, which are largely from Tlatilco and Las Bocas, although a few were purchased at Tlapacoya. The ware is black or brown, sometimes with excised or scraped zones, and the animal may be placed on an oblong or hat-box-shaped hollow base, decorated with scroll designs. The majority of such pieces show amusingly modeled and stylized ducks [55-58], of the *Spatula clypeata* species, the Northern Shoveller, which is the only Mexican duck with a long, spoon-shaped bill expanded at the end.[34] The Shoveller is a winter visitor to many parts of Mexico, including both central highlands and Gulf Coast; it is probably a young Shoveller that is carved on the front of Monument 9 at San Lorenzo. The Olmec were perhaps interested in this bird for its water associations.

Next in frequency among animal effigies is the fish. Stylized to the point of Disneyesque caricature, it is unrecognizable as to species [59, 60]. Of all the effigy vessels the finest shows a bird with upraised beak and tail; its beautiful black ware surface opposes polished to matte areas [61]. The eye has the Olmec flamebrow and the wing the same paw-hand motif found on the aviform monument from Laguna de los Cerros. The bird, which is probably represented in the act of drinking water, may not be entirely fantastic: the proto-type might be *Gymnostinops montezuma,* the Montezuma Oropen-dola, a strikingly large troupial of the Gulf Coast forests which is noted for building long nests in trees.

Effigies of mammals are rarer than those of birds and fish. Some cannot be surely identified and might be purely imaginary [62-65]. Nonetheless one can identify dogs, anthropomorphic coatimundis and opossums, and a magnificent rocker-stamped effigy in the

13

13   *Yuguito. Said to be from Tlatilco. Stone, 3½" high.*
      American Museum of Natural History, New York 30.2-8700

14

 14   Yuguito. Provenience unknown. Stone, 5¼" high.
Collection Alice and Nasli Heeramaneck, New York

15   Yuguito, were-jaguar face. Purchased at Tlatilco in 1953.
Stone, 4" high. Dumbarton Oaks, Washington, D. C. B-2.OS

16   Yuguito. Tlatilco. Stone, 5¾" high.
Museum of Primitive Art 64.35

15

16

Museo Nacional de Antropología in Mexico City represents a peccary.[35]

Reminiscent of certain Colima tomb figures are the effigies of animals, probably dogs [66, 67], with human faces and bottle necks in place of tails; these, like some of the smaller hollow human figures, have whistles in the head. Also basically bottle-shaped is an effigy parrot from Tlatilco [69], again pointing to a possible connection with the Pre-Classic tomb sculpture of western Mexico.

Las Bocas and Tlatilco have yielded bowls with lateral flanges reproducing the outlines of fish [70, 72] — head, fins, and tail. It is a kind of vessel which tends to be somewhat late in the Pre-Classic of other areas in Mesoamerica, being present in Monte Alban I, for instance, and may be somewhat tardy in the Tlatilco sequence as well. A Shoveller duck effigy from Tlapacoya [71] is in the same style.

Human effigy vessels accomplished in the same lively vein as the animals have been recovered from Tlatilco. Two show much the same subject [73, 74]: a fat, grotesque personage has one arm raised to the head, thus serving as a handle for the vessel, and the other clasped to the belly; the hair is carried out by a punctate appliqué. I believe that both of these figures are shown masked, the face set off from the head by braids of hair or fiber in the manner of figurines known to represent masked dancers (see below). The greatest piece in this genre is the rocker-stamped, squatting effigy figure from Tlatilco in the Museo Nacional de Antropología, also fitted with the same kind of mask.[36]

Other pottery figures, which could have been used as vessels, include the large-sized acrobats [75] with one foot placed on the head and the other open as a spout. A number of these have been found at Tlatilco, while a piece of unknown provenience, certainly from central Mexico and in the same style, is in the form of a grotesque man seated on a four-legged stool [76]. The hair on all the figures is indicated by roughening with a corn cob. The most extraordinary effigy vessel of all is one ascribed to Santa Cruz [77]: a white-slipped figure of a skeletonized old woman with hunchback, deformed legs, and open mouth serving as spout, certainly one of the most powerful examples of ceramic sculpture from pre-Columbian Mexico. The same theme is repeated in a small, solid figurine from Las Bocas [200].

Two small Tlatilco vessels are in the shape of human heads. One, a buffware with red pigment rubbed onto the roughened areas [78], is a highly modeled caricature of a bony-faced person with prominent cheekbones and full lips; it is an astonishing piece of characterization. Equally odd is a head with bland expression [79] and arms and legs closely attached. The "ears" are spouts linking it to the large "horned" figures. The back of this specimen is incised and excised with standard Tlatilco designs.

An object of unique interest is an extraordinary house or temple effigy vessel in the Leff collection [80] with a Tlatilco provenience. Basically a bottle with cubical lower chamber, the open-work walls and elaborate roof are exterior additions to the structure. The thatched roof represented here is perhaps tied with rope, while the upper part ends in a scroll-like crest. It is our only glimpse of how the structures of the Middle Pre-Classic might have looked.

The kinds of pottery from Middle Pre-Classic central Mexican sites in private collections or found by archaeologists are legion, and space is lacking to describe all this variation. The loop-handled incense burners from Tlatilco, for instance, can only be mentioned in passing. Since Tlapacoya is hardly known to scientific excavators, with the exception of Barba de Piña Chan's report[37] on a Proto-Classic tomb, it would be premature to attempt any serious classification of its pottery. Suffice it to say that some of it is different from anything known at Tlatilco, Gualupita, and Las Bocas, and probably can be placed somewhat later.

Pottery figurines

Untold numbers of solid clay figurines have been found at Tlatilco and other Pre-Classic sites in Mesoamerica. With the exception of mold-made specimens from the very late site of Chupícuaro in Guanajuato, all are modeled by hand. The bodies and heads were fashioned with the fingers; small fillets or strips were added; and maguey thorns or triangular or small oval stamps were utilized for details. After firing, red, black, and white pigments were applied in imitation of face- and body-painting.

In spite of the abundance of such figurines, their function remains unknown. Recognizable gods are notoriously absent, except those few representing the Fat God of ancient Mexico [148], with his pot belly and feathered costume. Since the majority are of young women, Sejourné[38] among others has suggested that they served as fertility images to ensure abundant harvests, but this does not explain the presence of male or androgynous figurines. The wide range of human activities — mothers with children, dancers, ball players, and musicians — implies a closer relation to secular life. Such figurines are included in some Tlatilco graves, and they are a typical feature of the burial furniture of various sites in Middle Pre-Classic central Mexico.[39] Were they perhaps attendants of some kind, in the manner of the tomb figures of Tang China? Could they have been "portraits" of living persons? We can do little more than speculate at this time.

Clarence Hay was the first to attempt a classification of the Pre-Classic figurines of Central Mexico; this was later refined by George Vaillant in the course of his excavations, when he was able to propose a stratigraphically defined chronological sequence for his types.[40] The Hay-Vaillant classification may be over-refined considering the relatively small sample with which they were working, and the stylistic overlap between their defined types. It was, nevertheless, a remarkable exercise in archaeological classification. We do not know what the contemporaneity of many of these types means: variation between local centers of manufacture, between families of artists, or between individual artists? There are entire groups of figurines which must have been made in a short period of time by a single craftsman, and it would not be impossible that they constitute "types" in themselves.

A rough chronology is as follows: probably the oldest in central Mexico is the Cañitas type [81-83],[41] not found in any of Vaillant's excavations, but present in collections ascribed by James Bennyhoff to the Tlálpan phase, a pre-El Arbolillo I manifestation

17

18

17   Head from a figure. Said to be from Tlatilco.
      Jade, 1⅝" high.
      Collection Mr. Aaron Furman, New York
18   Punch. Said to be from Tlatilco. Jade, 3⅛" long.
      Collection André Emmerich Gallery, New York

19   Bowl, were-jaguar profile designs.
      Morelos, site unknown, reported found with 21.
      White to buff, 4½" high.
      Collection Mr. and Mrs. D. Daniel Michel, Chicago
20   Straight-sided bowl, were-jaguar profile designs.
      Tlapacoya. White to buff, 6½" high.
      Collection Mr. Jay C. Leff, Uniontown, Pa.

at the site of Cuicuilco.[42] These are extremely simple, gingerbread-like figurines with eyes in the form of large holes surrounded by a circle of tiny punctations. Most are female, and double-headed examples are known. Cañitas figurines, which also come from the Tlatilco area, may well be Early, rather than Middle, Pre-Classic.

The Middle Pre-Classic villages excavated by Vaillant on the northwestern shore of the ancient Great Lake open the sequence with Type C1, C1-2, and C3 figurines, with the last-named the earliest. C figurines [84-89] could well be a development of the Cañitas type; all specimens show nearly nude females, with features made by filleting and punctation. The eyes are doubly-impressed blobs of clay. Turbans, necklaces, wristlets and anklets are appliquéd strips, and extensive body painting is indicated by post-fired designs in red, black, and white. These types are known at El Arbolillo, Zacatenco, and Tlatilco, with C1 figurines probably persisting beyond the end of the Middle Pre-Classic at Tlapacoya [90-92].

The ultimate refinement of the art of figurine-making in central Mexico is seen in the D1 [93-113] and D4 [114-127] types, which are among the most beautiful objects of their size in all of the New World. They are characteristic of Middle Pre-Classic Tlatilco and allied sites, but are absent from Late Pre-Classic sites like Ticoman; D4, which is a highly sophisticated variation of D1, is almost entirely confined to Tlatilco. The small arms, wasp waists, inflated thighs, and tiny vestigial feet of these figures give them a charm which is matched by the sophistication of facial features. A curious feature of D1 and D4 faces is that the eyes are identical with the mouth — extremely narrow lenticular slashes in the clay, with a tiny central

punctation carried out with the end of a thorn. The line of the brow is often a bow-shaped ridge; women's hair may be worn on the top of the head or in two braids carried down behind the ear spools to the shoulders. D4 figurines, the rarest and most valuable, have imaginatively treated bodies with greatly swollen thighs, wider and narrower eyes and mouth, and more use of post-fire polychroming.

The great majority of D1 and D4 figurines are female: young, shapely bodies and stylish faces are treated with amusing charm. There is more emphasis on full breasts than in most Pre-Classic figurines. The amount of ethnological detail given in these tiny objects is unusual. Besides elaborate body decoration, perhaps carried out with the use of roller stamps, women sometimes wore short skirts apparently made of grass or fiber [114]. A few rare figurines show scenes of maternity: a woman with child straddled on her hip [95, 99], or a woman holding a child in a cradle board [118]. In the latter it may be seen that fore-and-aft cranial deformation is being perpetrated on the soft skull of the infant, by tightly binding down the forehead with straps. Many adult skulls from the burials were so deformed.

Dancers in a variety of poses are also encountered in the D1 and D4 types; most are women. Some wear tiers of rattles on the legs [106] and occasionally on the wrists. These greatly resemble the strings of cocoons filled with pebbles worn on the legs of the modern Yaqui deer dancers in northwestern Mexico. Most interesting are the false face dancers [123, 124]; they are male and have faces covered by goateed masks possibly identical with those of pottery from Tlatilco and Las Bocas. One of these dancers also has rattles on the legs. They again recall the Yaqui Pascola dancers.

19

20

21 Straight-sided bowl, were-jaguar profile designs.
    Morelos, site unknown, reported found with 19.
    White to buff, 4³/₈″ high.
    Collection Mr. Raymond Wielgus, Chicago

22 *Straight-sided bowl, relief bird and scroll design.*
    Puebla, site unknown.
    Blackware, red and yellow pigment, 4½″ high.
    Museum of Primitive Art 56.157

23   *Tecomate, jaguar dragon (?) design. Las Bocas.*
      Blackware, 3³/₄" high.
      Collection Mr. and Mrs. Miles Lourie, New York

24   *Tecomate, excised design. Las Bocas.*
      Blackware, red pigment, 3³/₄" high.
      Collection Everett Rassiga Inc., New York

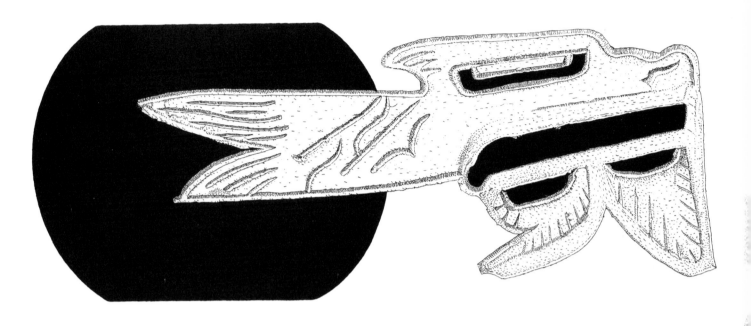

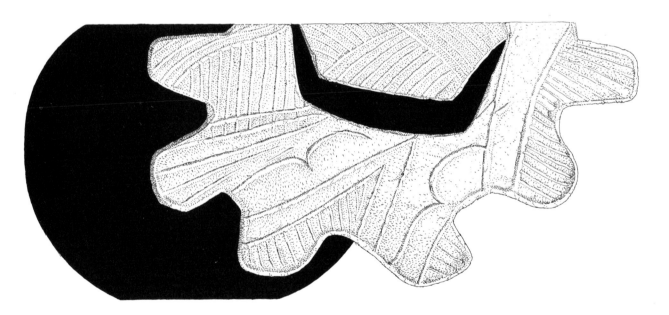

25 Bowl, relief "matting" design.
Las Bocas. Blackware, red pigment, 3½" high.
Collection Mr. Michael Kan, Berkeley

26 Straight-sided bowl, jaguar paw design.
Las Bocas. Blackware, 2⅝" high.
Collection André Emmerich Gallery, New York

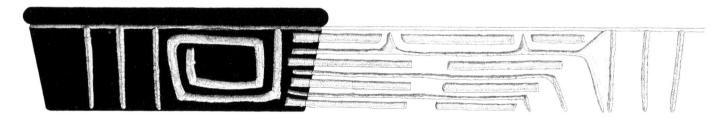

27   *Straight-sided bowl, stylized jaguar paw design.*
Las Bocas. White rimmed blackware, 9¹/₂″ diameter.
Collection Everett Rassiga Inc., New York

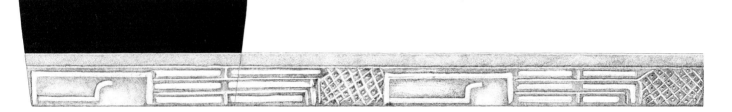

28   *Straight-sided bowl, jaguar spot (?) design.*
Tlapacoya. White to buff, 4⁷/₈″ high.
Collection Miss Judith Small, New York

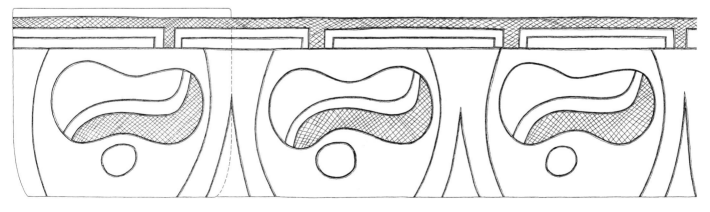

29 Developed design from a bowl, jaguar dragon and paw
design. Las Bocas. Blackware, red pigment, 2¹/₂" high.
Collection Mr. Jay C. Leff, Uniontown, Pa.

30 Developed design from a bowl, jaguar dragon design.
Las Bocas. Blackware, red pigment, 2¹/₂" high.
Collection Mr. and Mrs. D. Daniel Michel, Chicago

31 Developed design from a tecomate,
jaguar dragon and Olmec cross design.
Las Bocas. Greyware, 2⁷/₈" high.
Collection Mr. and Mrs. Arthur N. Seiff, New York

32 Bowl with thickened and everted rim, excised design.
Tlatilco. Blackware, 2¹/₄" high.
Collection Mr. Jay C. Leff, Uniontown, Pa.

33 Bowl with thickened and everted rim, excised design.
Las Bocas. White to buff, 1³/₄" high.
Collection Everett Rassiga Inc., New York

34 Bottle, relief scroll design around neck. Purchased
at Tlatilco in 1945. Blackware, red pigment, 7" high.
American Museum of Natural History, New York 30.2-9398

29

30

31

32

33

34

35   Bottle, openwork bottom. Las Bocas.
       Blackware, red pigment, 8⁵/₈″ high.
       Collection Mr. and Mrs. D. Daniel Michel, Chicago

36   Bottle, jaguar paw design. Las Bocas.
       Blackware, red pigment, 7³/₄″ high.
       Museum of Primitive Art 63.48

37   Bottles, incised designs. Tlatilco.
       Blackware, red pigment, 4″ high.
       Left: Collection Everett Rassiga Inc., New York
       Right: Essex Arts, New York

36

35

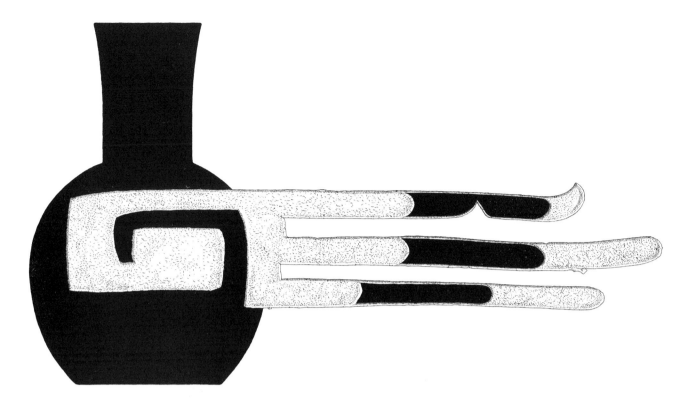

36 a

37

37 a

38 Bowl, zoned and incised design. Tlatilco.
Red on buff, 3¹/₂" high.
Collection Everett Rassiga Inc., New York

39 Three chambered bottle. Tlatilco.
Red on buff, 9⁷/₈" high.
Collection Everett Rassiga Inc., New York

40 Ring jar with female effigy neck. Tlatilco.
Red on buff, 8³/₈" high.
Collection Mr. Jay C. Leff, Uniontown, Pa.

38

39

41   *Composite bottle. Tlatilco. Brownware, 7¹/₂" high.*
      Collection Everett Rassiga Inc., New York

42   *Composite silhouette bowl. Tlatilco. Brownware, 3" high.*
      Museum of the American Indian, Heye Foundation,
      New York 22/5671

43   *Stirrup spout bottles. Tlatilco.*
      Red on buff, 7⁵/₈" and 3⁵/₈" high.
      Museum of the American Indian, Heye Foundation,
      New York 22/9286 and 22/4694

41   42

43

44

45

44   Bottle with effigy neck. Excavated at Tlatilco, 1947-49.
      Brownware, 7¼" high.
      Chicago Natural History Museum 240546

45   Gadrooned bottle. Excavated at Tlatilco, 1947-49.
      Red on buff, 11⅜" high.
      Chicago Natural History Museum 240545

46   Bottle in the form of a foot. Provenience unknown.
      Red on buff, 9⅝" high.
      Peabody Museum of Archaeology and Ethnology,
      Harvard University, Cambridge 35-106-20/13137

46

43

47   Gadrooned bowl. Tlatilco. Whiteware, 3″ high.
Collection Everett Rassiga Inc., New York

Another male rôle represented by rare D1 figurines is that of ball player [111]. As already noted, one from Burial 129 at Tlatilco wears hand, knee, and ankle guards, and has what seems to be a thick or padded loin cloth. Some males peer from elaborate helmets and resemble astronauts [108, 109]. They are probably ball players also, as are the figurines with the lower part of the faces covered [100], drawing an analogy to the protective helmets of Late Classic Maya figurines of ball players from Lubaantun in British Honduras.[43]

Women playing end flutes, holding dogs [88], or engaged in many other activities are known [107]. Beyond the genre scenes are the monstrosities, and perhaps witch doctors, which show up in D1 and other central Mexican figurine types. The usual kind of freak has two heads and one body [136]; a fairly common figurine has a composite face [103, 104], with three eyes, two noses, and one mouth, or variations on this theme.

More frequent in Tlatilco graves than D1 and D4 is the D2 type [128-134], broadly similar in concept but far less interesting in execution and content. The fillets which set off the slanting eyes of D1 figurines become accentuated, while the bodies are flatter and quite standard of pose, usually standing. The most stylized of all the Middle Pre-Classic figurines are Type K [135-140]. Placed in the same Tlatilco graves as D1, D4, and D2, they are coeval yet markedly different. They are so unlike the former that they may have been made outside the Valley of Mexico, possibly in Morelos; their extremities are treated as the large, hollow D-K figures of the Río Cuautla area, to which Covarrubias thought they were ancestral. K figurines are distinguished by their large, goggly eyes formed by impressing clay pellets with an oval instrument. Most are female, although a few composite animal figurines and double-headed monsters are known.

Not represented at Tlatilco and most primarily Middle Pre-Classic sites, but abundant at Tlapacoya is Type C4 [144-146], also said to have a distribution in Puebla and Morelos.[44] Probably later in time than the Middle Pre-Classic, C4 does not occur at Ticoman and must be early in the Late Pre-Classic. In style it is a flamboyant development of the C tradition, with small gingerbread-cookie bodies but very large, coiffured heads that are sometimes tilted back. The eyes are rounded, flat lumps which occasionally have shallow, double impressions in each. A better made and rather well polished C4 variant at Tlapacoya has punched eyes [146].

There is a wide and highly varied miscellany of figurines which has not been mentioned here: they are either so rare or so atypical that they cannot be considered representative of main stream folk tradition in central Mexico during the Pre-Classic. A further kind of figurine which is reasonably frequent — Olmec or Olmecoid — will be discussed in a subsequent section. It lies very much outside this folk tradition.

In summary, the distribution of handmade figurines suggests that there were local centers of manufacture specializing in certain types, that some (like D4 at Tlatilco) never diffused beyond their point of origin, but that others were traded to distant points in regional markets. I think it unlikely that they had much religious function beyond serving as company for the dead in a future life, and for that reason they represented the good things of this life, like

48

49

50

51

52

53

54

55
Duck on scroll decorated base.
Las Bocas. Blackware, 8¼" high.
Collection Mr. Jay C. Leff, Uniontown, Pa.

56
Duck with removable head. Tlatilco.
Buffware, traces of red pigment, 2" high.
Collection Mr. Jay C. Leff, Uniontown, Pa.

57
Duck. Tlapacoya. Buffware, 5" high.
Collection Mr. Charles B. Cohn
and Mr. Stuart P. Anderson, Allston, Mass.

58
Duck. Tlatilco. Greyware, 6³/₈" high.
Collection Mr. and Mrs. Miles Lourie, New York

59
Fish on scroll decorated base. Las Bocas.
Blackware, traces of red pigment, 8" high.
Collection Mr. Jay C. Leff, Uniontown, Pa.

60
Fish with "spout in mouth." Las Bocas.
Blackware, red pigment, 7" high.
Collection Everett Rassiga Inc., New York

55   56

57

58

61 *Bird on scroll decorated base,*
    excised jaguar paw designs on wings. Las Bocas.
    Blackware, 10¼" high.
    Collection Mr. Jay C. Leff, Uniontown, Pa.
62 *Figure (monkey?) on decorated base.*
    Tlatilco. Blackware, red pigment, 2⅝" long.
    Collection Mr. Jay C. Leff, Uniontown, Pa.
63 *Monkey? Tlatilco. Greyware, 2" high.*
    Collection Everett Rassiga Inc., New York
64 *Bound coatimundi. Tlatilco. Buffware, 6½" high.*
    Collection Mr. Jay C. Leff, Uniontown, Pa.
65 *Animal? Tlatilco. Greyware, 6" high.*
    Collection Everett Rassiga Inc., New York

61

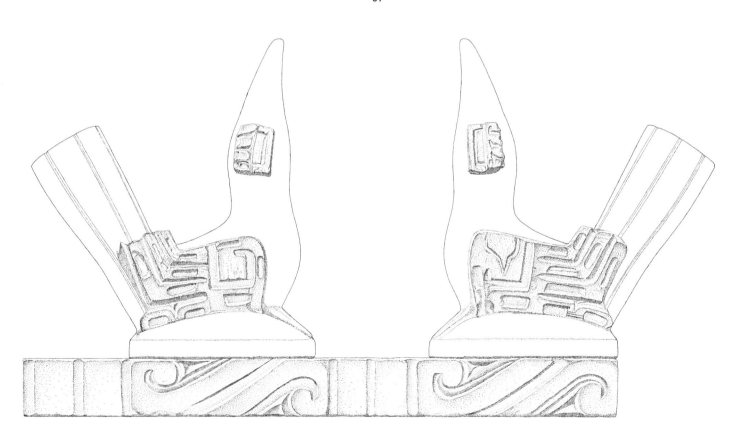

62

63

64

65

pretty women. Lastly, untouched, as many other aspects of Pre-Classic art in central Mexico, by the Olmec tradition, they were indicative of the indigenous styles of the region before the Olmec influx.

Tlapacoya ball players

One group of figurines deserves separate mention: these are of men wearing more elaborate ballcourt paraphernalia than that seen on D1 figurines [151, 152, 157, 158]. All examples thus far can be traced to Tlapacoya, and they are not easy to type in the Hay-Vaillant scheme, but seem to be late forms of Type C. Details are built up with appliqué strips. There are thick, probably protective, bands on arms, wrists (or hands), knees, and ankles. Circling each figure is a wide, heavy belt which protrudes toward the front; on the midline in front is a circular object, usually concave, which may represent the concave mirrors worn by Olmec nobles, placed on a background of vertical or crossing bands. Pads dangle over the hips, hanging from this close approximation of the yoke-like belts worn by ball players of the Classic period. As on some D1 figurines, a few of the ballplayers wear small masks over the lower part of the faces [157, 158]. Those without such ornament are crowned by towering and distinctive headdresses [152].

The Tlapacoya ball players conclusively demonstrate that by the start of the Late Pre-Classic the rubber ball game of Mesoamerica had taken its typical form in the highlands. The D1 figurines prove it present in the Middle Pre-Classic.

Pottery masks

The masks of Pre-Classic Mexico speak with a directness possessed by few objects from this epoch [161-169]. In late pre-Conquest times, masks were worn by god-impersonators during calendrical festivals, but they may not have so functioned in an earlier era. Pottery masks chosen to be interred with the dead have been found in graves at Tlatilco, Las Bocas, and Tlapacoya.

Their small size, 4 to 6 inches in height, forces the erroneous conclusion that they were not masks at all. The clay figurines prove, however, that they were meant to be worn over the lower part of the face only, the mummer peering over the top edge of the mask. A few of the larger ones, on the other hand, covered the entire face, but all are less than life size. The clay examples from central Mexico are not mere replicas of wooden originals: they are all pierced for suspension, and thus were functional.

The usual type of pottery mask is almost circular, and convex. Eyes and mouth are cut out and edged by ridges of clay, producing a Haniwa-like face, and punctate or incised tabs stand for ears and hair. Often a tongue protrudes from the lower part of the mouth.

There are many variations on this type, and a wide assortment of grotesque forms which in some cases approach the terrifying. One extraordinary piece from Tlatilco shows a wrinkled old man with mouth twisted upward as though a victim of a stroke [163]. From Las Bocas comes a beautifully modelled and burnished mask of an ape-like person with pursed lips, heavy brow-ridges and prominent cheek-bones [164]. In the collection of masks from Tlatilco in the

Museo Nacional de Antropología are pop-eyed grotesque faces with bulging lower lips; a partly skeletal jaguar face; and a face split down the center line, one side a human skull and the other a staring visage with protruding tongue.[45]

Do they represent gods? Certainly the deities of the Olmec tradition are missing, such as the were-jaguar of the magnificent wooden mask from Cañon de la Mano, Guerrero.[46] Unfortunately, we do not know the gods representative of the indigenous folk tradition of Pre-Classic central Mexico. As mentioned previously, there are striking similarities to masks worn by modern Pascola dancers among the Yaqui Indians of Sonora; these men are ceremonial hosts during festivities and act as ceremonial clowns as well. Their main rôle is as dance specialists, and the deer dancer, the most famous of all, wears leg rattles and adopts poses which are amazingly like those seen on Tlatilco figurines. I think it not unlikely that the Pre-Classic masks were worn principally by persons playing such rôles. It is also clear that ballplayers could be so masked, perhaps during the post-game festivities. Finally, the use of masks, on the testimony of the figurines, seems to have been confined to men.

Roller stamps

Clay roller stamps [170-173], often misleadingly called "cylinder seals," are found in almost all Pre-Classic sites in Mesoamerica. Small flat stamps of clay are also known, and were manufactured until the Spanish Conquest, but roller stamps probably died out with the beginning of the Classic. The principal, and perhaps only use, of such stamps must have been to apply pigments—red, black, yellow, and white—to the skin. Type D figurines indicate how highly polychromed the well-painted female must have been in Middle Pre-Classic times. Designs on face and body are usually geometric; roller stamps were well adapted to such a purpose—many are slightly concave on the outer surface—and all are pierced longi-tudinally so that a stick could be used in the rolling process. From the pigment still adhering to most stamps, cinnabar or red ochre was the most popular color.

There may well have been a functional subdivision among flat stamps and cylindrical rollers. The former could have been confined to decorating the face, as those in the shape of human footprints. Footprints are seen painted on the lower faces of some Tlatilco figurines.[47] Roller stamps, on the other hand, often reach a large size, up to 7 or 8 inches in length, and would have been more suitable for use on body surfaces.

The Olmec presence is strong in the boldly executed relief designs of the roller stamps from Tlatilco and Las Bocas. In particular, the Olmec hand-paw design is prominent [173]; others show conven-tionalized ducks [174] or purely geometric patterns [175] which may have some esoteric Olmec meaning. More specifically related to the iconography of the Olmec "heartland" is a design showing a bird with hand-paw wing [172].

Human effigy figures

Large, hollow pottery figures which are not functional vessels are common in the burial furniture of Tlatilco and are contemporary

66

67

68

with Type D figurines and the pottery types associated with them [176-183]. A magnificent example of these figures, decorated with *chapopote* (asphalt) paint, was found in a site of the Late Ajalpan period in the Tehuacán Valley of Puebla, and MacNeish believes, contrary to the usual opinion, that small, solid figurines may have been presaged by the large, hollow ones.[48]

The most striking type is found at Tlatilco, but is particularly common at Santa Cruz and other sites in the Río Cuautla drainage of Morelos. These standing figures are female, with large heads, very small flipper-like arms, small breasts, and large, pierced navels. Eyes are treated like those of D1 or D2 figurines, and the extremities like Type K: they are sometimes called D-K figures. The headdress is usually pill-box-shaped, but one from Tlatilco has an expanded-conical hat [176]. Slipped in red, red-and-black, or plain burnished, these figures reach heights of 27 inches and are thus the largest ceramic objects in Pre-Classic Mexico. Variations on the theme of the Río Cuautla type occur at Tlatilco

and Santa Cruz [179], but sometimes lack the Type K treatment of the extremities. Often seated figures, the headdress or hairdo is rounded with raised panels. Two grotesque objects in this vein, both of unknown provenience, are a female with a small goatee [183], and a pair of "Siamese twins" sharing one of their legs [182]. Achondroplasia is probably represented in a distinct class of hollow female figures from Tlatilco, with very large heads, tiny limbs, and swollen thighs. "Horned" figures come from Tlatilco [180] and Gualupita,[49] and are considerably smaller than the Río Cuautla type. In large part they are similar to the less K-like variants discussed above, but have two wide, spout-like projections on the top of the head. The limbs are short and tapered.

As in the case of the smaller, solid figurines, there is little basis for speculation about the use of these objects; one can point out that these larger, hollow figures are restricted to representations of women.

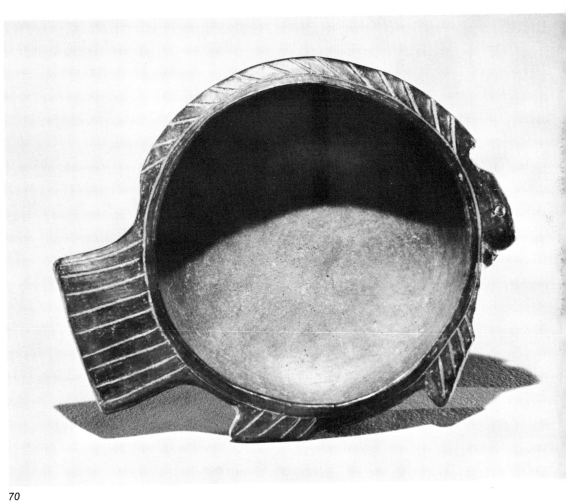

69

70

71

72

73

74

71 Bowl in the shape of a duck. Tlapacoya.
Greyware, 3¼″ high.
Collection Mr. Jay C. Leff, Uniontown, Pa.

72 Open bowl in the shape of a fish. Tlatilco.
Buffware, traces of red pigment, 8¼″ long.
Collection Everett Rassiga Inc., New York

73 Masked figure with hand to head.
Tlatilco. Red on buff, 6¾″ high.
Collection Everett Rassiga Inc., New York

74 Masked figure with hand to head.
Tlatilco. Red on buff, 5¼″ high.

75 Acrobat. Tlatilco. Redware, 15½″ high.
Collection Mr. Proctor Stafford, Los Angeles

76 Seated figure on a stool. Provenience unknown.
Redware, 14″ high. Private collection

77 Kneeling skeletonized figure. Santa Cruz.
White to buff, 6⅜″ high. Private collection

75

76

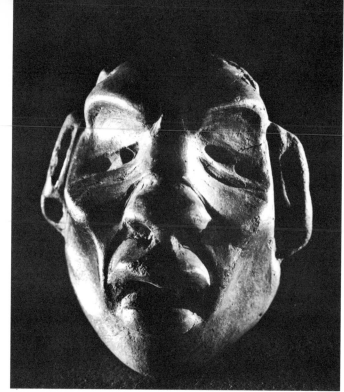

78

78   Human head vessel. Tlatilco.
      Buffware, red pigment, 3³/₄" high.
      Collection Everett Rassiga Inc., New York
79   Head vessel. Tlatilco. Buffware, 3" high.
      Collection Mr. Jay C. Leff, Uniontown, Pa.
80   House or temple. Tlatilco.
      Mottled white to buff, 8¹/₂" high.
      Collection Mr. Jay C. Leff, Uniontown, Pa.

79

79 a

81

82

83

84

85

86

87

88

89

90

91

92

81 Standing figure (Cañitas type).
Tlatilco. Buffware, 4" high.
Collection Mr. Jay C. Leff, Uniontown, Pa.

82 Standing figure (Cañitas type). Tlatilco.
Buffware, 3⁵/₈" high. Museum of the American Indian,
Heye Foundation, New York 22/708

83 Standing figure (Cañitas type).
Tlatilco. Buffware, 3³/₈" high.
Collection Everett Rassiga Inc., New York

84 Standing figure (type C1).
Tlatilco, reported found with 85, 86, and 87.
Red and black paint, 5¹/₄" high.
Museum of the American Indian, Heye Foundation,
New York 23/4614

85 Standing figure (type C1).
Tlatilco, reported found with 84, 86, and 87.
Red and black paint, 5¹/₄" high.
Collection Mr. and Mrs. Leon Meadow, New York

86 Standing figure (type C1).
Tlatilco, reported found with 84, 85, and 87.
Red and black paint, 5¹/₈" high.
Collection Miss Rea Goodman, New York

87 Standing figure (type C3).
Tlatilco, reported found with 84, 85, and 86.
Traces of yellow paint, 6" high.
Collection Mr. and Mrs. Miles Lourie, New York

88 Standing figure holding dog (type C3).
Tlatilco. Traces of red and white paint, 4¹/₂" high.
Collection Everett Rassiga Inc., New York

89 Seated figure (type C3). Tlatilco. Red paint, 2¹/₂" high.
Collection Everett Rassiga Inc., New York

90 Standing figure (type C1). Tlapacoya.
Red pigment, 8¹/₂" high.
Collection Everett Rassiga Inc., New York

91 Standing figure (type C1). Tlapacoya.
Red pigment, 7¹/₂" high.
Collection Everett Rassiga Inc., New York

92 Standing figure (type C1). Tlapacoya.
Red pigment, 7⁵/₈" high.
Collection Everett Rassiga Inc., New York

93 Standing figure (type D1). Tlatilco.
White and red paint, 5³/₈" high.
Collection Mrs. McClure Capps, Los Angeles

94 Standing figure (type D1). Tlatilco.
White and red paint, 4¹/₂" high.
Collection Mrs. Aaron Furman, New York

95 Standing figure with child (type D1).
Tlatilco. Traces of red and yellow paint, 3¹/₄" high.
Collection Everett Rassiga Inc., New York

96 Standing figure (type D1). Tlatilco. Buffware, 3¹/₈" high.
Collection Alice and Nasli Heeramaneck, New York

97 Standing figure with hole through chest (type D1).
Tlatilco. Traces of yellow and red paint, 5" high.
Collection Mr. Jay C. Leff, Uniontown, Pa.

98 Standing figure (type D1).
Tlatilco. Yellow paint, 4³/₄" high.
Collection Everett Rassiga Inc., New York

93

94

95

96

99

97

98

101

102

100

99   Seated figure with child (type D1).
      Tlatilco. Traces of red and yellow paint, 2³/₄" high.
      Collection Everett Rassiga Inc., New York

100   Masked figure, ballplayer? (type D1).
      Tlatilco. Traces of yellow and white paint, 5³/₈" high.
      Collection Mr. and Mrs. D. Daniel Michel, Chicago

101   Standing figure (type D1). Tlatilco.
      White to yellow slip, 5¹/₂" high.
      Collection Mr. Jay C. Leff, Uniontown, Pa.

102   Standing figure (type D1). Tlatilco.
      Traces of white paint, 7⁵/₈" high.
      Collection Mr. Jay C. Leff, Uniontown, Pa.

103   Double-faced figure (type D1). Tlatilco.
      Red and yellow paint, 3⁵/₈" high.
      Collection Everett Rassiga Inc., New York

104   Double-faced figure (type D1). Tlatilco.
      Red and yellow paint, 3³/₄" high.
      Collection Mr. Jay C. Leff, Uniontown, Pa.

105   Standing figure (type D1). Tlatilco.
      Red and yellow paint, 4¹/₄" high.
      Museum of Primitive Art 61.155

106   Standing figure (type D1). Tlatilco.
      Red and yellow paint, 4³/₈" high. Private collection

107   Four figures seated in a circle (type D1). Tlatilco.
      Yellow paint, 3¹/₂" high.
      Collection Everett Rassiga Inc., New York

108   Standing figure, ballplayer? (type D1). Tlatilco.
      Red, white and yellow paint, 3⁷/₈" high.
      Collection Mr. Jay C. Leff, Uniontown, Pa.

109   Standing figure, ballplayer? (type D1). Tlatilco.
      Red, white, and yellow paint, 4¹/₄" high.
      Collection Everett Rassiga Inc., New York

110   Standing figure (type D1). Tlatilco.
      Red, white and yellow paint, 4¹/₄" high.
      Collection Everett Rassiga Inc., New York

103   104

105

106

107

108

109

110

111

112

113

111   *Bearded figure carrying a ball (type D1). Tlatilco.*
      Red and yellow paint, 2⁷/₈" high.
      Collection Mr. Jay C. Leff, Uniontown, Pa.

112   *Seated figure (type D1). Tlatilco.*
      Red and yellow paint, 3³/₄" high.
      Collection Mr. and Mrs. Miles Lourie, New York

113   *Three seated figures with holes in their heads (type D1).*
      Tlatilco.
      Traces of yellow paint, 4¹/₃, 4³/₄, and 5³/₄" high.
      Collection Mr. Jay C. Leff, Uniontown, Pa.

114   *Standing figure (type D4). Tlatilco.*
      Black, red and yellow paint, 4" high.
      Collection Everett Rassiga Inc., New York

115   *Standing figure (type D4). Tlatilco.*
      Red, white and purple paint, 3³/₄" high.
      Museum of Primitive Art 61.157

116   *Standing figure (type D4). Tlatilco.*
      Red, white and yellow paint, 4" high.
      Collection Everett Rassiga Inc., New York

117   *Standing figure (type D4). Tlatilco.*
      Red and yellow paint, 4¹/₄" high.
      Collection Mr. Jay C. Leff, Uniontown, Pa.

118   *Seated figure with child in cradle board (type D4).*
      Tlatilco. Red, white and yellow paint, 2⁵/₈" high.
      Collection Mr. Proctor Stafford, Los Angeles

114

115

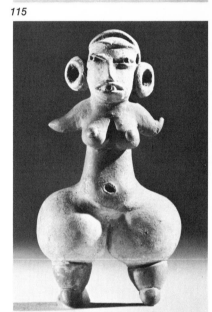

116

117

118

119 Standing figure (type D4). Tlatilco.
     Red, white and yellow paint, 4¼" high.
     Collection Mr. and Mrs. Miles Lourie, New York

120 Standing figure (type D4). Tlatilco.
     Red and yellow paint, 4" high.
     Collection Mr. and Mrs. Miles Lourie, New York

121   *Standing figure (type D4). Tlatilco.*
       Red and yellow paint, 5" high.
       Collection Everett Rassiga Inc., New York

122   *Standing figure (type D4). Tlatilco.*
       Red, white and yellow paint, 5" high.
       Collection Everett Rassiga Inc., New York

123   Masked figure (type D4). Tlatilco.
      Red paint, 3⅝" high.
      Collection Everett Rassiga Inc., New York
124   Masked figure (type D4). Tlatilco.
      Red paint, 4" high.
      Collection Mr. Jay C. Leff, Uniontown, Pa.
125   Seated figure (type D4). Tlatilco.
      Red and yellow paint, 2⅞" high.
      Collection Mr. Jay C. Leff, Uniontown, Pa.
126   Standing figure (type D4). Tlatilco.
      Red and yellow paint, 4" high.
      Collection Everett Rassiga Inc., New York
127   Standing figure with feline face (type D4). Tlatilco.
      Red and white paint, 3" high.
      Collection Mr. Frank Elmer, New York
128   Standing figure (type D2). Tlatilco.
      Buffware, 5" high.
      Collection Mr. and Mrs. Miles Lourie, New York
129   Standing figure (type D2). Tlatilco.
      Red paint, 5⅝" high.
      Museum of Primitive Art 61.151
130   Standing figure (type D2). Tlatilco.
      Red paint, 5½" high.
      Collection Everett Rassiga Inc., New York
131   Standing figure carrying ball? (type D2). Tlatilco.
      Buffware, 4¼" high.
      Collection Everett Rassiga Inc., New York
132   Standing figure with child (type D2). Tlatilco.
      Buffware, 4¼" high.
      Collection Everett Rassiga Inc., New York
133   Seated figure (type D2). Tlatilco.
      Red paint, 2¾" high.
      Collection Mr. Jay C. Leff, Uniontown, Pa.
134   Standing figure (type D2). Tlatilco.
      Red pigment, 4⅞" high.
      Collection Mr. Jay C. Leff, Uniontown, Pa.

123

124

125

126

127

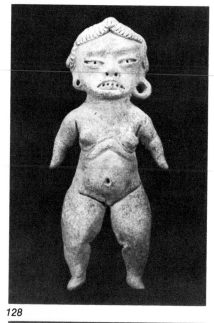

128

128a

129

130

133

134

131

132

135 *Dog with dog (type K). Tlatilco.*
   White paint, 2³/₄" high.
   Collection Mr. Jay C. Leff, Uniontown, Pa.
136 *Double-headed figure (type K). Tlatilco.*
   Yellow, red and white paint, 3³/₄" high.
   Collection Mr. Jay C. Leff, Uniontown, Pa.
137 *Seated figure (type K). Tlatilco.*
   Buffware, 5¹/₈" high.
   Collection Mr. Jay C. Leff, Uniontown, Pa.
138 *Standing figure (type K). Tlatilco.*
   Yellow, red and white paint, 3³/₈" high.
   Collection Everett Rassiga Inc., New York
139 *Seated figure (type K). Tlatilco.*
   Yellow, red and white paint, 3" high.
   Collection Everett Rassiga Inc., New York
140 *Standing figure with child (type K). Tlatilco.*
   Yellow, red and white paint, 4" high.
   Collection Mr. and Mrs. Miles Lourie, New York

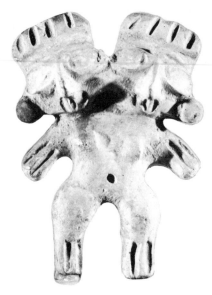

136

137

135

138

141 Standing figure (type D-C9). Tlatilco.
Traces of yellow paint, 4¾" high.
Collection Everett Rassiga Inc., New York

142 Standing figure (type D-C9). Tlatilco.
Yellow paint, 4½" high.
Collection Everett Rassiga Inc., New York

143 Standing figure (type D-C9). Tlatilco.
Red and yellow paint, 4⅝" high.
Museum of Primitive Art 61.153.

144 Standing figure (type C4). Tlapacoya.
Greyware, 5" high.
Collection Mr. and Mrs. Miles Lourie, New York

145 Standing figure with child (type C4). Tlapacoya.
Greyware, black paint, 6¼" high.
Collection Everett Rassiga Inc., New York

146 Seated figure (type C4). Tlapacoya.
Buffware, 4¼" high.
Collection Mr. Jay C. Leff, Uniontown, Pa.

147 Masked dancer with rattles around legs. Tlatilco.
Buffware, red, and yellow paint, 7⅞" high.
Collection Mr. Jay C. Leff, Uniontown, Pa.

148 "Fat god" figure. Tlatilco. White pigment, 5⅝" high.
Collection Mr. Jay C. Leff, Uniontown, Pa.

149 Vessel in the form of an old woman. Tlatilco.
Red pigment, 3⅜" high.
Collection Mr. Jay C. Leff, Uniontown, Pa.

150 Masked dancer with rattles around legs. Tlatilco.
Buffware, red and yellow paint, 8" high.
Collection Mr. and Mrs. Daniel Michel, Chicago

151 Masked figure with tall headdress and ballgame "belt."
Tlapacoya.
Remainder of red, yellow and white pigment, 8⅜" high.
Collection Everett Rassiga Inc., New York

139

140

141

142

143

144

145

146

147

148

149

150

151

152

152 a

153

154

155

156

157

158

152   *Figure with tall headdress and ballgame "belt." Tlapacoya.*
      White slip, 7" high.
      Collection Everett Rassiga Inc., New York

153   *Standing figure. Tlapacoya. White slip, 5¹/₂" high.*
      Collection Everett Rassiga Inc., New York

154   *Standing figure. Tlapacoya. White slip, 4¹/₂" high.*
      Collection Mr. and Mrs. Arthur N. Seiff, New York

155   *Standing figure. Found at Tlatilco.*
      White slip, red pigment, 3³/₈" high.
      Collection Everett Rassiga Inc., New York

156   *Standing figure. Tlapacoya, found with 162.*
      White slip, 3³/₄" high. Private collection

157   *Masked figure with ballgame "belt." Tlapacoya.*
      White slip, 5¹/₈" high. Private collection

158   *Masked figure with ballgame "belt." Tlapacoya.*
      White slip, 6¹/₂" high.
      Collection Miss Judith Small. New York

159   160

159   *Hunchback. Tlapacoya.*
      Greyware, black paint, 3³/₄" high.
      Collection Everett Rassiga Inc., New York

160   *Hunchback. Tlapacoya.*
      Greyware, black paint, 3⁷/₈" high.
      Collection Everett Rassiga Inc., New York

161   *Mask. Tlatilco. Red pigment, 6" high.*
      Collection Mr. Thomas Ford, Boston

162   *Mask. Tlapacoya, found with 156.*
      Red-brown slip, 4" high. Private collection

163   *Mask. Tlatilco. Buffware, red pigment, 4³/₄" high.*
      Collection Mr. Jay C. Leff, Uniontown, Pa.

164   *Mask. Las Bocas. Greyware, 5¹/₂" high.*
      Collection Mr. Jay C. Leff, Uniontown, Pa.

161

162

163

164

165   *Mask. Tlatilco.*
Buffware, red and yellow pigment, 5" high.
Collection Mr. and Mrs. Miles Lourie, New York

166   Mask. Tlatilco.
Buffware, red and black pigment, 6" high.
Collection Mr. Jay C. Leff, Uniontown, Pa.

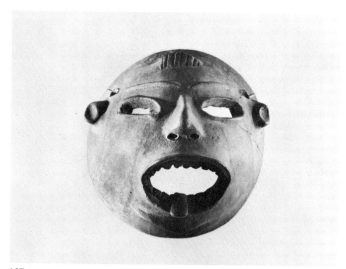

167

168

167　Mask. Tlatilco.
　　Mottled buffware, red paint, 4¹/₂" high.
　　Collection Mr. Michael Kan, Berkeley
168　Mask. Tlatilco. Buffware, red paint, 4" high.
　　Collection Mr. and Mrs. Arthur N. Seiff, New York

169

169   *Mask. Tlatilco. Buffware, red paint, 5¼" high.*
Museum of Primitive Art 63.31

170

171

172

173

170 *Roller stamps. Las Bocas. Buffware, 3¼″ and 2⅞″ high.*
Left: Museum of Primitive Art 65.1
Right: Collection Everett Rassiga Inc., New York

171 *Roller stamps. Las Bocas.*
Buffware, traces of red paint, 2⅝″ to 3″ high.
Private collection

172 *Roller stamp, bird with wing as paw design. Las Bocas.*
Buffware, 3½″ high.
Collection Mr. and Mrs. D. Daniel Michel, Chicago

173 *Roller stamp, stylized paw design. Tlatilco.*
White on buff, 5″ high.
Collection Mr. Jay C. Leff, Uniontown, Pa.

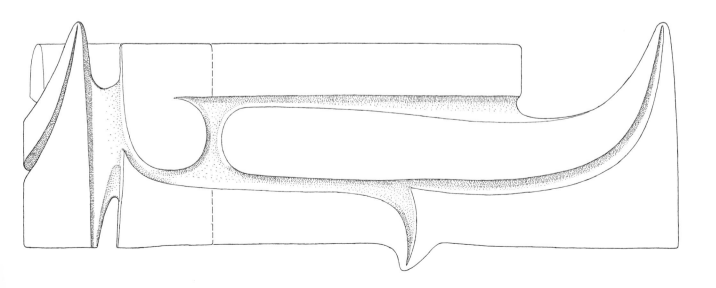

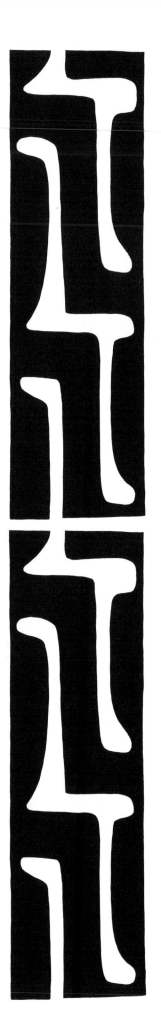

176

174 *Developed roller stamp design. Tlatilco. 3¹/₂" wide.*
Museum of the American Indian, Heye Foundation,
New York 22/4686

175 *Developed roller stamp design. Tlatilco. 3¹/₂" wide.*
Collection Mr. Jay C. Leff, Uniontown, Pa.

176 *Standing figure with conical hat. Tlatilco.*
Black on red, 24" high.
Collection Mr. and Mrs. D. Daniel Michel, Chicago

177 *Standing figure with hat. Tlatilco. Buffware, 27" high.*
Collection Mr. Jay C. Leff, Uniontown, Pa.

178   *Standing figure. Tlatilco.*
Mottled buffware, red pigment, 20" high.
Collection Mr. Stanley Selengut, New York

179   *Standing figure. Santa Cruz. Redware, 18¼" high.*
Collection Mrs. Jacob M. Kaplan, New York

180	Seated "horned" figure. Tlatilco.
	Buffware, white and red paint, 8½" high.
	Collection Mr. and Mrs. Albert B. G. Iardella, New York

181	Seated figure. Tlatilco.
	Black on red, white pigment, 11¼" high.
	Collection Mr. Jay C. Leff, Uniontown, Pa.

180

181

182   *Double figure. Provenience unknown.*
Red on buff, 11½″ high.
Collection Mrs. Bernard F. Gimbel, Greenwich, Conn.

183 Standing figure. Provenience unknown.
Red on buff, 14" high.
Collection Mr. Jay C. Leff, Uniontown, Pa.

The "Jaguar's Children"

Olmec style and iconography have been shown to be present in jades, on *yuguitos,* on pottery vessels, and on most of the roller stamps, but above all it is manifest in the magnificent white-ware figures and figurines of Tlatilco, Las Bocas, Tlapacoya, Gualupita, and Atlihuayán.

These are the "Jaguar's Children": Olmec were-jaguar babies, offspring of feline father and human mother, deities of thunder, lightning, and rain. Nude and often sexless, their obesity is that of eunuchs, while their expressions and slanting eyes give a strong impression of some condition like mongolism. Their jaguar ancestry shows only in the down-drawn corners of the mouth.

The finest examples of the supreme Olmec deity from central Mexico are the large, hollow seated figures. Two were excavated by the Vaillants in the Gualupita cemetery [186] and although mutually dissimilar they share the same treatment of the eyes with double impressions.[50] Burial 162 at Tlatilco produced two hollow white-ware seated Olmec figures,[51] associated with D1 figurines and a flaring-necked jar; these are inferior in artistic value and workmanship to a marvellous example of the genre in the Feuchtwanger collection.[52]

A particularly important hollow Olmec figure was found at Atlihuayán, in Morelos. It is significant because the seated personage, besides having were-jaguar features, wears over head and back the skin of a more feline were-jaguar with flame-brows and the typically Olmec hand-paws.[53]

The recently discovered Las Bocas has produced the greatest "Jaguar's Children." Clearly the products of individual artists of exceptional talent, they are nude and sexless or of doubtful gender, and sit with legs apart. One, grotesquely corpulent, sucks a fore-finger with head thrown back [184], in the characteristic pose of a five-month to year-old infant. The closefitting cap evokes the "helmets" of the colossal heads and is decorated with raised punctate disks, curvilinear zones filled with red pigment, and a vertical zone on the back carved as though tattooed or painted. The other equally splendid piece from Las Bocas is in the Leff collection [185] and stares fixedly forward with somewhat crossed eyes; the bald head, and admittedly oriental expression, recall some Chinese Lohan.

Most of the hollow, white-ware Olmec figures from Tlapacoya are inferior to the best ones from Las Bocas and Tlatilco with one exception. This is the remarkable figure in the Leff collection [190], seated cross-legged with head slightly tilted to one side in a most naturalistic pose. The sex of this individual is again equivocal; the body either has small breasts or is merely fat. In beauty of expression it is the rival of Leff's Las Bocas figure, and if it were not for the different character of the clay and slips from which both were fashioned, one might think them the products of the same artist or workshop. The remainder of the Tlapacoya pieces in this class are cruder in every respect, and much less sophisticated. One hand is occasionally raised to the head [189], as in the more indigenous human effigy vessels from Tlatilco, and the bodies may be stylized in the same direction as the stubby-limbed hollow figures of Pre-Classic central Mexico [187].

The small pottery figurines in Olmec style at Las Bocas [193-199] are of the same fine, white-paste clay that was used in Kaolin ware (which may have originated in western Puebla). In delicacy of feeling they are the best of their class, with finely-modeled were-jaguar baby features, polished surfaces, and bright red pigment applied to matte or punctate zones. A surprising range of poses can be seen among them: crosslegged, reclining with head raised on one hand, head resting on an arm supported on a knee, and so forth. The reclining examples [199] closely resemble the Olmec jade figurines erroneously said to be dancing. Besides the material, workmanship, and pose, Las Bocas Olmec figurines can be identified by the treatment of the eye, which usually is a simple, shallow, horizontal slit without punctation. The most unusual example of the type is in the Wielgus collection: an enormously fat little Olmec person [193] who can hardly cross his legs from his corpulence, and who wears a peaked cap. It may be an attempt to show the Fat God, and there is a resemblance to the pot-bellied sculptures from Monte Alto on the Pacific Coast of Guatemala which have Olmecoid features. Some of the standing Olmec figurines of Las Bocas are more in line with female Tlatilco types and might fall within Vaillant's Type A if the clay from which they were manu-factured was not so dissimilar.

From Tlapacoya comes a series of figurines of singularly large dimensions, ranging in height from 5⅝ to 17 inches. They all have Olmec or Olmecoid were-jaguar baby faces, and are either bald or wear a fringed coiffure or headdress that is quite different from those of Las Bocas. In the treatment of the legs they are reminiscent of Type D2 figurines, but the worn white slip, overall proportions, and lack of artistic excellence puts them in a class by themselves, probably somewhat late in the Pre-Classic sequence.

184 *Seated figure with finger in mouth. Las Bocas.*
    Whiteware, red pigment, 13" high.
    Museum of Primitive Art 65.28
185 *Seated figure. Las Bocas.*
    Whiteware, red pigment, 12" high.
    Collection Mr. Jay C. Leff, Uniontown, Pa.
186 *Seated figure.*
    Gualupita, excavated by George Vaillant in 1932.
    Remainder of cream slip, 11" high.
    American Museum of Natural History, New York 30.1-2847

184 a

184 b

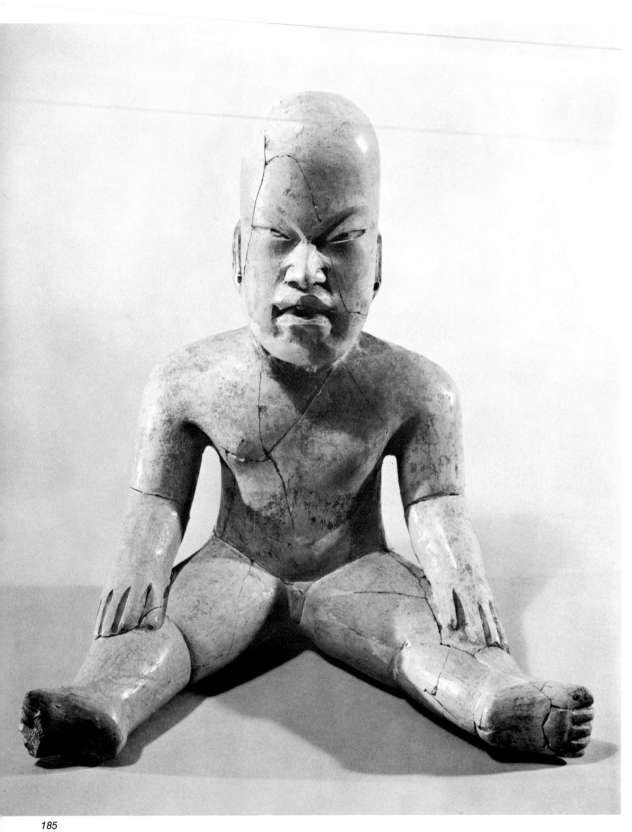

185

186

187

188

189

190   *Seated figure. Tlapacoya. White slip, 6¹/₂″ high.*
        Collection Mr. Jay C. Leff, Uniontown, Pa.
191   *Seated figure. Tlapacoya.*
        Remainder of cream slip, red pigment, 9¹/₈″ high.
        Collection Origins, Boston
192   *Seated figure. Tlapacoya.*
        Mottled white to buff, black paint, red pigment, 10¹/₂″ high.
        Collection Mr. Gunnar Didrichsen, Helsinki, Finland

190   191   192

193

193 a

193   *Seated figure. Las Bocas. White slip, 4³/₈'' high.*
    Collection Mr. Raymond Wielgus, Chicago

194   *Seated figure. Las Bocas.*
    White slip, red pigment, 3³/₄'' high.
    American Museum of Natural History, New York T109/227

195   *Seated figure. Las Bocas.*
    White slip, red pigment, 2³/₄'' high.
    Collection Mr. Jay C. Leff, Uniontown, Pa.

196   *Seated figure. Las Bocas.*
    White slip, red pigment, 3⁵/₈'' high.
    Collection Everett Rassiga Inc., New York

197   *Seated figure. Las Bocas.*
    White slip, red pigment, 3⁷/₈'' high.
    Collection Everett Rassiga Inc., New York

198   *Seated figure. Las Bocas.*
    White slip, red pigment, 3³/₄'' high.
    Collection Everett Rassiga Inc., New York

199   *Reclining figure. Las Bocas.*
    White slip, red pigment, 4³/₄'' long.
    Collection Mr. Jay C. Leff, Uniontown, Pa.

194

195

196

197

198

199

200

201

202

203

204

205   "Winged" figure. Las Bocas. Buffware, 5¹/₈" high.
Collection Mr. Jay C. Leff, Uniontown, Pa.

207   Standing figure. Las Bocas. Red on buff, 7³/₄" high.
Collection Everett Rassiga Inc., New York

206   Standing figure. Las Bocas. Red on buff, 5³/₄" high.
Collection Mr. Jay C. Leff, Uniontown, Pa.

THE OLMEC PRESENCE IN CENTRAL MEXICO

Although there may be differences of opinion among authorities over the details of Pre-Classic chronology, they agree that before the Ticoman period there was an impressive flowering of central Mexican culture in which powerful Olmec influence can be detected. This influence makes itself felt in Middle Zacatenco times, particularly toward the end of the phase at the Tlatilco cemetery. In effect, as has often been noted, there are manifestly two distinct artistic traditions during the Middle Pre-Classic in the highlands, one Olmec and the other indigenous. The latter, probably drawn from the native peasant cultures of El Arbolillo, Zacatenco, and other small farming villages of the region, is expressed in Middle Pre-Classic times in pottery figurines, clay masks, certain kinds of vessels, and in a lively, bold style which tends towards the grotesque and humorous.

What is the explanation for the Olmec presence? If one adopted Piña Chan's hypothesis of Olmec origins, placed by him in central Mexico, specifically in the state of Morelos,[54] the task would be simplified. However, it seems difficult to derive the three-dimensional Olmec sculptural style from Chalcatzingo, the only site in central Mexico with Olmec stone carving. With one exception there are only reliefs, themselves probably derived from prototypes in the Gulf Coast "heartland."

This subject of Olmec origins is a difficult one. Miguel Covarrubias leaned to Guerrero's Pacific Coast region, where Olmec-style jades are frequently encountered. He argued that since the larger-scale monuments are totally absent in that zone, one would expect the style to have arisen there.[55] This argument was based on the wholly unwarranted assumption that small-scale always precedes large-scale art. On the contrary, it is held by most students that the Gulf Coast of southern Veracruz and western Tabasco was the Olmec "heartland." The great florescence of Olmec art plus the full range of the iconography, so central to the culture, is completely expressed only here. I think this last point is the most significant, for the claim that "biggest is oldest" may also be little more than an unverified assumption. There is overwhelming evidence that Olmec culture and art crystallized in the "heartland" during the Middle Pre-Classic, and towards the latter part of that period spread to the highlands of central Mexico.

Covarrubias called the Olmec "invaders," and concluded that they must have been a theocratic élite ruling the simple Zacatenco-like village peoples in the highlands, supposedly paving the way for the "theocratic" civilizations of the Classic period.[56] It was a Marxist-style theory of the struggle for power among contending classes leading to the establishment of the state. Others, adopting a more idealistic stance, have seen Olmec missionaries from the "heartland" spreading the cult of the were-jaguar to central Mexico, to Guerrero, and down the Pacific coast to El Salvador. These two viewpoints are by no means in conflict, as successful missionary work has often been accomplished with the sword, usually as an *ex post facto* justification for imperial expansion and enslavement.

It is here proposed that the problem of Olmec diffusion be looked at in a slightly different light. First, was there ever an Olmec "theocracy," or for that matter, such a form of government anywhere in pre-Conquest Mesoamerica? Theocracies, defined as a "government or state governed by God directly or through a sacerdotal class," are exceedingly rare at any time or place in the world, and tend not to be self-perpetuating. With the possible exception of the Zapotecs at Mitla as described by Burgoa in a somewhat fanciful account,[57] none of the Late Post-Classic states were so organized. It is foolhardy to assume that the civilizations of the Classic and Pre-Classic had a type of state completely different from that of the Post-Classic. Such a supposition is invalidated by the recent work of Proskouriakoff on the inscriptions of the Classic Maya (always given a priest-ridden government in the archaeological literature): the ancient Maya, as among most early civilizations, were ruled by secular lords who drew their power from lineage and from conquest.[58] Why then, should the important personages on the Olmec monuments be "priests?" The wearing of a were-jaguar mask may not have been the mark of a sacerdotal specialist, but the outward and visible symbol of profane power; especially so, if the Olmec rulers claimed divine descent from the were-jaguar, as the Aztec monarchy claimed descent from Quetzalcoatl as justification for rulership. God-masks are worn by many of the royal politicians in the Mixtec codices.

A more mundane explanation of the Classic and Pre-Classic states of Mesoamerica allows structural continuity between the earliest—the Olmec, and the latest—the Aztec. I do not believe the Aztec were very different from all the peoples who preceded them in central Mexico. We know how Aztec power—economic, religious and military—was spread in Mexico prior to the Spanish Conquest; the records are as detailed as any for a Mesoamerican civilization. The abundance of documents for the proto-historic period makes the Post-Classic look dissimilar to the Classic. In my opinion this is an illusion—we simply know more about the Post-Classic.

As described by Sahagún, the Aztec expansion went hand-in-hand with two kinds of movements of scarce goods: long-distance trade, and tribute. Trade was carried out by a distinct hereditary caste called the *pochteca,* who occupied their own ward in the cities of the Valley of Mexico, and who had their own internal political organization under the direct authority of the emperor.[59] These long-distance traders were outside the market system of the Aztec cities, operating only in foreign lands with which there might or might not be commercial treaties. If there were none, the traders went, in disguise or armed, as hostilities might break out at any moment with the natives; they served as both spies and *agents provocateurs,* for the Aztec emperor was quick to declare war on any state which had maltreated his *pochteca.* The ostensible object was to bring from distant markets, some of which were protected "ports of trade" in buffer states, luxury goods such as amber, precious feathers, or gold, all unavailable or scarce within the Aztec realm, for the use of the royal palace.

The transformation of a foreign state into a province of the Aztec empire was often a rapid one. There were armed "vanguard merchants" among the *pochteca* who could, and sometimes did, conquer cities; more usually, the Aztec army invaded an area which had been provoked by the *pochteca.* In either case, the territory was quickly set up as an Aztec province with a military garrison. What was once long-distance trade became enforced tribute, with the addition of surprising amounts of food needed to feed the rapidly expanding population of the Aztec capital.

The institution of the *pochteca* is probably very old in Meso-america. The god of the *pochteca,* Yacatecuhtli, goes back as far as the Early Classic at the site of Teotihuacán.[60] I suggest that institution is even more ancient, that it arose to meet the needs of royal power in the Olmec state of the Middle Pre-Classic. This might explain the Olmec presence outside the "heartland." Specifically, it is proposed that the Olmec ruling class, in its rôle as the allocator of scarce goods in a redistributive economy, had certain needs for rare raw materials and other luxuries which could only be met by long-distance trade beyond the frontiers of the Olmec state, and that a professional trading class satisfied these needs, carrying the culture and art style, along with Olmec religion, to remote lands.

The substance which the Olmec royal power must have desired above all was jade, followed by serpentine. Neither of these are naturally available on the Gulf Coast. Foshag has shown that jade is developed *in situ* in serpentine veins which usually have outer zones of chlorite schist and black amphibolite.[61] No such formations could exist in the "heartland." To date, the only known jade deposits in Mesoamerica are at Manzanal in the Motagua Valley of Guatemala, probably the source of Classic Maya jade. Significantly, serpentine veins occur in an area near Tehuitzingo, Puebla, only 25 miles south of Las Bocas; Foshag comments that the serpentine there is distinctly antigoritic in character like that used in Olmec figurines, and he mentions a group of ancient mounds at the foot of the formation. Southwestern Puebla, and perhaps neighboring Morelos, could have been the source of Olmec serpentine.

It has long been noted that there are probably more Olmec jades from the Pacific coast and Balsas River basins of Guerrero than from all the rest of Mexico put together. Could Guerrero itself have been the source of the raw material and of many of the worked objects in Olmec style? Metamorphic chlorite schists of late Paleozoic and Mesozoic age are extensively distributed around the Taxco region of northern Guerrero; there are also Paleozoic metamorphic formations over much of the lower Balsas. Chances are good that deposits of the blue-green jade so prized by the Olmec will be found in Guerrero some day.

The developing Olmec state on the Gulf Coast could have known about such sources, and sent *pochteca* groups out to barter with the chiefs of these foreign territories for jade and serpentine. They might well have established Chalcatzingo as a *pochteca* center with warehouses to collect serpentine and other products traded from neighboring peoples. Various areas along the Balsas and coastal Guerrero may have been "ports of trade" visited by the Olmec *pochteca,* for which Guerrero artisans supplied both raw jade and finished works of art in the Olmec taste. Rubín de la Borbolla has pointed out that such a practice may have continued into Classic times, when local carvers were producing stone masks for the Teotihuacán trade.[62] If these figurines and small *objets de vertu* were being carried back to the "heartland" by fast-moving groups of *pochteca,* this might explain the near absence of Olmec jade and serpentine objects in Tlatilco and Las Bocas burials.

A glimpse into what other products might have been exchanged between Gulf and Pacific coasts is afforded by the Codex Mendoza,

the Aztec tribute list. [63] Besides sizeable amounts of jade beads, Guerrero at the time of the Conquest was the major supplier of copal incense to the Aztec state. Tochtepec, a province which included part of the Olmec "heartland," tributed with 18,000 rubber balls, 100 pots of fragrant liquid amber resin, and 24,000 bunches of tropical bird feathers. Morelos, parenthetically, supplied pottery and bark paper in quantity. The mention of such a large number of rubber balls recalls the traditional role of the lower Gulf Coast as the source of that item. It suggests that ball game equipment may have been the principal goods carried by the Olmec *pochteca* to barter with central Mexican and Guerrero artisans for fine jade and serpentine.

This could explain the Olmec presence in central Mexico in the Middle Pre-Classic. This important region lay athwart what might have been a jade-serpentine route, the Mexican counterpart of the great Amber Route which played such an important part in bringing Mediterranean civilization to central and northern Europe. The establishment of centers of armed *pochteca* over this route and as far south as Chalchuapa, El Salvador, could have brought commercial prosperity to much of Mesoamerica. It could have also resulted in the annexing of distant areas to the Olmec state. It most certainly brought to a number of peasant cultures the cult of the were-jaguar, the divine power of the Olmec civilization.

*208   Hunchback. Las Bocas. Redware, 3½" high.
Collection Mr. Jay C. Leff, Uniontown, Pa.*

NOTES

1 Sears, 1952; Coe, 1962, pp. 26-7.
2 Vaillant, 1930, 1931, 1935a.
3 Vaillant, 1935b, p. 303-4.
4 Vaillant and Vaillant, 1934.
5 Vaillant and Vaillant, 1934, p. 59.
6 For the history of how "Olmec" came to be recognized as a culture, see Coe, 1965, and Squier, 1964. For a full bibliography of Olmec art, see Jones, 1963.
7 Covarrubias, 1943, 1950; Moedano Koer, 1957; Piña Chan, 1958; Romano, 1962, 1963.
8 Covarrubias, 1943, p. 43.
9 Squier, 1964, contains a full description of the Tres Zapotes and La Venta excavations.
10 Stirling, 1940.
11 Guzman, 1934.
12 Piña Chan, 1955a.
13 Barba de Piña Chan, 1956.
14 There is a detailed justification of this scheme in Coe, 1961, pp. 120-130.
15 Porter, 1953; Piña Chan 1958.
16 Paul Tolstoy, personal information. In a multilithed paper received too late for inclusion in this study, Tolstoy scrupulously examines all of the possibilities suggested by the Tlatilco burials.
17 Porter, 1953.
18 Coe, 1961, pp. 130-2.
19 Stirling, 1955, pp. 19-20, pls. 25, 26a.
20 Covarrubias, 1957, pl. 19.
21 Stirling, 1955, pls. 17, 18.
22 This monument is not illustrated in Medellín Zenil, 1960.
23 Stirling, 1943, pl. 36.
24 Guzman, 1934; Piña Chan 1955a.
25 Covarrubias, 1957, pl. 11.
26 Stirling, 1940, fig. 7.
27 Guzman, 1934, figs. 11-13.
28 Drucker, Heizer, and Squier, 1959, pl. 52 a-c.
29 Peterson and Horcasitas, 1957.
30 Porter, 1953, pl. 4d.
31 Illustrated in Marquina, 1951, lám. 68, lower right.
32 Porter, 1953, pl. 6 e, f.
33 Porter, 1953, p. 89.
34 Blake, 1953, p. 53.
35 Porter, 1953, pl. 9h.
36 Covarrubias, 1957, pl. 6, upper left.
37 Barba de Piña Chan, 1956.
38 Séjourné, 1952.
39 They are absent, however, in the graves of Zacatenco and El Arbolillo.
40 Vaillant, 1935b, pp. 291-302.
41 Covarrubias, 1957, pl. 7, lower right.
42 The Tlálpan phase collections were kindly shown to me by James Bennyhoff in September, 1964.
43 Joyce, 1933, pl. 7-8.
44 Vaillant, 1930, pl. 14 and p. 107.
45 Piña Chan, 1955b, lám. 19, 20, 27, 28.
46 Coe, 1962, pl. 21.
47 A foot-shaped flat stamp from Tlatilco is illustrated in Porter, 1953, pl. 13c; and a D1 figurine head with footprints on either cheek can be seen in Piña Chan, 1955b, fig. 10 (lower left).
48 MacNeish, 1964, p. 11, and personal communication.
49 Vaillant and Vaillant, 1934, fig. 14, 1.
50 Vaillant and Vaillant, 1934, fig. 14, 2-3.
51 Covarrubias, 1950, plate facing p. 153.
52 Covarrubias, 1957, pl. 1, lower left (wrongly captioned).
53 Piña Chan and López, 1952, fig. 3. No final report has yet appeared on these excavations, but the site has produced Dark Channeled ware, D1 figurines, and other materials indicating its close relationship to Gualupita and Tlatilco.
54 Piña Chan, 1955a, pp. 26-27; 1955b, pp. 106-107. An excellent summary of the problem of Olmec origins is given in Drucker, Heizer, and Squier, 1959, pp. 253-9.
55 Covarrubias, 1956, p. 15; 1957, pp. 76-7.
56 Covarrubias, 1957, pp. 77, 83.
57 Burgoa, 1934.
58 Proskouriakoff, 1961, p. 60.
59 A particularly complete description of the pochteca system is given in Book 9 of Sahagún, 1959; an excellent summary and interpretation of the role of the pochteca in the Aztec economy is by Chapman, 1957.
60 Séjourné, 1959, pp. 30-7.
61 Foshag, 1957, pp. 11-12.
62 Rubín de la Borbolla, 1964, pp. 13-16.
63 Barlow, 1949, which is a "translation" and analysis of the tribute lists given in the Codex Mendoza.

REFERENCES CITED

Barba de Piña Chan, Beatriz
1956   Tlapacoya; un sitio preclásico de transición.
       Acta Anthropológica, época 2, v. 1, no. 1.

Barlow, R. H.
1949   The extent of the empire of the Culhua Mexica.
       Ibero-Americana, no. 28.

Blake, E. R.
1953   Birds of Mexico. Chicago.

Burgoa, Fr. Francisco de
1934   Geográfica descripcion. 2 vols. Mexico.

Chapman, Anne M.
1957   Port of trade enclaves in Aztec and Maya
       civilizations. Trade and Market in Early Empires,
       ed. K. Polanyi et al., pp. 114-153. Glencoe.

Coe, Michael D.
1961   La Victoria, an early site on the Pacific coast
       of Guatemala. Papers of the Peabody Museum,
       Harvard University, v. 53.
1962   Mexico. New York.
1965   The Olmec style and its distributions.
       Handbook of Middle American Indians,
       v. 2, article 29. Austin.

Covarrubias, Miguel
1943   Tlatilco, Archaic Mexican art and culture.
       Dyn, The Review of Modern Art, nos. 4-5, pp. 40-46.
1950   Tlatilco: el arte y la cultura preclásica del
       Valle de México. Cuadernos Americanos, v. 51,
       no. 3, pp. 149-62.
1957   Indian Art of Mexico and Central America.
       New York.

Drucker, Philip, Robert F. Heizer, and Robert Squier
1959   Excavations at La Venta, Tabasco, 1955.
       Bureau of American Ethnology, Bulletin 170.

Foshag, William F.
1957   Mineralogical Studies on Guatemala Jade.
       Smithsonian Miscellaneous Collections,
       v. 135, no. 5.

Guzman, Eulalia
1934   Los relieves de las rocas del Cerro de la Cantera,
       Jonacatepec, Mor. Anales del Museo Nacional
       de Arqueología, Historia y Etnografía,
       época 5, v. I, pp. 237-51.

Jones, Julie
1963   Bibliography for Olmec sculpture.
       Primitive Art Bibliographies, no. 2, New York.

Joyce, T. A.
1933   The pottery whistle-figurines of Lubaantun.
       Journal of the Royal Anthropological
       Institute, v. 63, pp. xv-xxv.

MacNeish, Richard S.
1964   The origins of New World civilization.
       Scientific American, v. 211, no. 5, pp. 3-11.

Marquina, Ignacio
1951   Arquitectura prehispánica. Mexico.

Medellín Zenil, Alfonso
1960   Monolitos inéditos olmecas.
       La Palabra y el Hombre, no. 16, pp. 75-97.

Moedano Koer, Hugo
1957   Informe preliminar sobre los exploraciones
       arqueológicas de San Luis Tlatilco.
       Anales del Instituto Nacional de
       Antropología e Historia, v. 9, pp. 73-84.

Peterson, Fredrick, and Fernando Horcasitas
1957   Recent finds at Tlatilco.
       Tlalocan, v. 3, no. 4, pp. 363-5.

Piña Chan, Roman
1955a Chalcatzingo, Morelos. Informes, no. 4. Instituto Nacional
       de Antropología e Historia. Mexico.
1955b Las culturas preclásicas de la Cuenca de México.
       Mexico.
1958   Tlatilco. 2 vols. Mexico.

Piña Chan, Roman, and Valentin Lopez G.
1952   Excavaciones en Atlihuayán, Morelos.
       Tlàtoani, v. 1, no. 1, p. 12.

Porter, Muriel N.
1953   Tlatilco and the Pre-Classic cultures of the New
       World. Viking Fund Publications in Anthropology, no. 19.

Proskouriakoff, Tatiana
1961   The lords of the Maya realm.
       Expedition, v. 4, no. 1, pp. 14-21.

Romano, Arturo
1962   Exploraciones en Tlatilco, Mexico.
       Boletín del Instituto Nacional de Antropología e Historia,
       no. 10, pp. 1-2.
1963   Exploraciones en Tlatilco. Boletín del
       Instituto Nacional de Antropología e Historia, no. 14,
       pp. 11-13.

Rubín de la Borbolla, Daniel
1964   Escultura precolombina de Guerrero. Mexico.

Sahagún, Fr. Bernadino de
1959   Florentine Codex. Book 9—The Merchants.
       (Translated by C. E. Dibble and A. J. O. Anderson).
       Salt Lake City.

Sears, Paul B.
1952   Palynology in southern North America.
       I: Archaeological Horizons in the Basins
       of Mexico. Bulletin of the Geological Society
       of America, no. 63, pp. 241-254.

Séjourné, Laurette
1952   Una interpretación de las figurillas del arcaico.
       Revista Mexicana de Estudios
       Antropológicos, v. 13, pp. 49-63.
1959   Un palacio en la Ciudad de los Dioses
       (Teotihuacán). Mexico.

Squier, Robert J.
1964   A reappraisal of Olmec chronology.
       Ph.D. dissertation in Anthropology,
       University of California, Berkeley.

Stirling, Matthew W.
1940   An Initial Series from Tres Zapotes, Vera Cruz,
       Mexico. Contributed Technical Papers,
       Mexican Archeology Series, v. 1, no. 1.

1943 Stone monuments of southern Mexico.
Bureau of American Ethnology, Bulletin 138.

Vaillant, George C.

1930 Excavations at Zacatenco. American
Museum of Natural History, Anthropological
Papers, v. 32, pt. 1.

1931 Excavations at Ticoman.
American Museum of Natural History,
Anthropological Papers, v. 32, pt. 2.

1935a Excavations at El Arbolillo.
American Museum of Natural History,
Anthropological Papers, v. 35, pt. 2.

1935b Early cultures of the Valley of Mexico.
American Museum of Natural History,
Anthropological Papers, v. 35, pt. 3.

Vaillant, Susannah B. and George C. Vaillant

1934 Excavations at Gualupita.
American Museum of Natural History,
Anthropological Papers, v. 35, pt. 1.

Manufactured in the United States of America
Text: Sanders Printing Corporation, New York
Jacket: Drum Lithographers, Inc., New York
Composition: Empire Typographers, Inc., New York
Binding: Russell-Rutter Co., Inc., New York